All About
DAY
TRADING

OTHER TITLES IN THE "ALL ABOUT" FINANCE SERIES

All About
DAY
TRADING

THE EASY WAY TO GET STARTED

JAKE BERNSTEIN

New York   Chicago   San Francisco   Athens   London
Madrid   Mexico City   Milan   New Delhi
Singapore   Sydney   Toronto

1 2 3 4 5 6 7 8 9 0   QFR/QFR   1 9 8 7 6 5 4 3

ISBN   978-0-007-177860-2
MHID   0-07-177860-8

e-ISBN   978-0-07-177861-9
e-MHID   0-07-177861-6

This publication is designed to provide accurate and authoritative information in regard to the subject matter covered. It is sold with the understanding that neither the author nor the publisher is engaged in rendering legal, accounting, securities trading, or other professional services. If legal advice or other expert assistance is required, the services of a competent professional person should be sought.
>   —From a Declaration of Principles Jointly Adopted by a Committee of the
>   American Bar Association and a Committee of Publishers and Associations

Library of Congress Cataloging-in-Publication Data

Bernstein, Jacob.
   All about day trading / by Jake Bernstein.
     pages cm
   ISBN 978-0-07-177860-2 (alk. paper) — ISBN 0-07-177860-8 (alk. paper)   1. Day trading (Securities)   2. Futures.   3. Futures market.   I. Title.
   HG4515.95.B4677 2013
   332.64—dc23   2013006950

McGraw-Hill Education books are available at special quantity discounts to use as premiums and sales promotions or for use in corporate training programs. To contact a representative, please visit the Contact Us pages at www.mhprofessional.com.

This book is printed on acid-free paper.

Although it would seem that lower commissions, faster order execution, rapid dissemination of information, and advanced trading analysis software would combine to contribute to greater success and more profits for investors and traders, I do not believe that this has been the case. High-frequency trading, dark pools, and insider trading and have given the distinct edge to professional traders who have been able to game the system and gain a decided advantage over the average individual. It is becoming more difficult to make money, even with the advanced tools that we have. I believe that it is possible to have a more level playing field, provided we are educated in proper procedures and effective trading methodologies. Accordingly, the information in this book is directed toward that end, and I dedicate this book to the many thousands of day traders to come to the game with great ambition, a measure of hope, and optimistic expectations. If my trading structure and tools can bring positive outcomes to even a small percentage of those who read this book, then I feel I will have contributed some good to a business that has brought so much good to me. Clearly, what I teach, what I use, and what I have learned are not sure things; but they have structure, good logic, and objectivity—all of which contribute meaningfully to bottom-line success. I welcome constructive feedback and questions from my readers.

CONTENTS

Chapter 11

Chapter 12

Chapter 13

Chapter 14

Chapter 15

Chapter 16

Chapter 17

Chapter 18

Chapter 19

LIST OF TABLES

ACKNOWLEDGMENTS

Many thanks to those who assisted me in the process of writing this book. Although I have written many books, the process does not become easier, but my work is always facilitated by those who have skills that far exceed mine when it comes to the English language. My editors create clarity and find the right words for ideas that I am unable to express clearly. Accordingly I thank Zach Gajewski, associate acquisitions editor at McGraw-Hill, for his arduous efforts and persistence in editing my often unclear and confusing writing. Additionally, David Andrews, managing editor at Print Matters, Inc., was a joy to work with—making my often laborious task almost enjoyable, given his patience and well-appreciated sense of humor.

Finally, a special word of thanks to the great folks at Genesis Financial Technologies, www.GenesisFT.com, for permission to use their charts and indicators in this book.

The Lure, the Myth, and the Magic

Some have called it gambling. Others have called it an educated guess. The more optimistic refer to it as the last bastion of capitalism. Promoters and brokers with a vested interest have called it an outstanding way to make money. Occasionally it has been referred to as quasi-science. Some have even gone so far as to refer to it as unethical or even immoral. But no matter what you believe and no matter what you may say, whether positive or negative, the day trading game is here to stay.

Having phased through various iterations over the years, day trading today is not at all what it used to be. Price movements that once took several months to complete now happen in a matter of seconds. High-frequency trading is the most recent development, which, it has been estimated, accounts for over 60 percent of stock market trading volume on any given day.

As trading and investing have moved rapidly into the age of electronic order entry and execution, the lower cost of commissions as well as the increased speed of order execution have created highly favorable conditions for day trading opportunities. Never before have day traders enjoyed the ability to profit as handsomely from their efforts as they do today. Whereas such opportunities were once the domain of the professional, the average investor can now seize opportunities that were once available only to those on the inside of the trading game. The ability to use advanced trading software to analyze market trends and to then place orders and have them executed in a matter of seconds has lured many new investors and traders into the game in stocks, futures, Forex, and options. While the positives are obvious and available to anyone with the risk capital and a computer, every front has a back and the backside of this front is not without risk.

Opportunities abound and risks lurk beneath the surface. Those with a vested interest in promoting day trading—the media, the stock and commodity exchanges, brokerage firms, and those who purport to provide profitable trading advice and strategies—have done a remarkable job of promoting day trading. Nevertheless, they have fallen woefully short of acquainting newcomers with the risks. It is virtually impossible to avoid the numerous television and print ads promoting the virtues of Forex trading, day trading, electronic trading, and futures trading. Furthermore, the exchanges have done a very poor job of helping traders learn how to trade successfully. I often wonder why.

It would seem that with all of the quantum advances in computer technology, the ability to analyze market opportunities with sophisticated software, the low cost of commissions, and the rapid dissemination of news, the advantage to the investor would clearly show itself in bottom-line profits. My impression is, however, that this is not the case. In fact I would guess—and this is only a guess—that the average investor, as well as the newcomer to day trading, is primarily a loser in this high-stakes game. Sadly, the technology that has enabled professional traders to make money has not enabled the unsophisticated investor to profit. They are grist for the mill and generally continue to lose, most likely at a more rapid pace than ever. I have no hard and fast statistics to support my contention, but having presented seminars and hosted several hundred webinars throughout the world, and having been a keynote speaker at numerous investment conferences, I've had the opportunity to meet the public and to hear their tales of woe. I have also enjoyed personally mentoring about one thousand traders and can speak from considerable experience about what I have seen in the average day trader.

You may think it peculiar that I begin a book on day trading with such concern and seemingly bad news. There is a method to my madness. My goal for over four decades in the trading business has been to create wealth for myself and those who avail themselves of my educational opportunities, trading methods, and strategies. I am well acquainted with the opportunities. I am also well acquainted with the risks. All too often the industry in which I'm involved emphasizes the profit potential more than the risk of loss. I want to compensate for that by issuing sufficient "health warnings."

There is no doubt that there are numerous opportunities and rags to riches stories about trading. There is no doubt that record market volatility during the course of the day (by which I mean large price swings) has created more profit potential than ever before. But here is the rub: profit potential in no way equates to bottom-line profits. In every business there are rules, procedures, strategies to minimize losses, strategies to maximize profits, many do's and don'ts, operational procedures, and organizational issues. Not a single promotional piece I have seen in the media emphasizes the necessity of understanding these vital details.

Just this morning I saw an advertising piece on CNBC, the most widely broadcast and followed cable business television show in the world, offering trading software with "a strategy you can start using today." I scratched my head and wondered where the rest of that promise was. *The mere fact that you can use a strategy today says nothing about its potential profitability.* The mere fact that you get something for free when you buy a particular program tells you nothing about how well the program has worked. You don't know how much risk and effort is involved and whether the strategy provides clear, objective, actionable, and potentially profitable opportunities that are not subject to interpretation. I can give you a gun, but if you don't know how to use it you can shoot yourself or someone else. Furthermore, you may have gotten a defective gun.

I find myself in a peculiarly uncomfortable situation. As I begin my 44th year in the trading and investing business, I see a glaring lack of skill and valid information in the critical areas that facilitate success for the average trader and investor. The failure is not in the lack of available information but rather in the quality of information and the lack of emphasis on the importance of such information. By information I mean the exact details of how to make money at the day trading game. There are relatively few individuals who are either willing or able to provide such education to the average investor. That is one of the things I will attempt to do in this book.

So what is all the fuss about? The fuss is about the opportunity and the potential for profit. The fuss is about the fact that it is now easier than ever before to be profitable. The fuss is about the fact that price movements or swings, otherwise known as volatility, within the course of the day is huge. The fuss is about the fact that orders can be placed virtually anytime from anywhere at the lowest commission ever. The fuss is about the promise of profits while the dark side, namely the potential for losses, is generally ignored. It is my goal to help bring light to the dark side through education, clarity, and clearly defined procedures. In so doing I will banish from the trading kingdom some of the words and ideas that have been embraced by so many traders for so long. I will not talk to you about "looks like" or "seems to me" or "this might be," or any other terms that are conditional in the sense that they require interpretation. Interpretation is a function of perception. Perception is a function of your internal wiring. Perception is a function of who you are, how you were raised, what you think you see, what you want to see, what kind of a day you've had, how you feel at the moment, and what you want to believe. Perception can also be a function of hope. As traders and investors, we need to banish hope from the kingdom. Hope clearly indicates insecurity, and insecurity indicates a lack of confidence in the trading methodology we're using.

But I'm getting ahead of myself. Let's get back to what all the fuss is about. Let's get back to a clear understanding of why this book has been written and what you as a current or aspiring day trader can do to improve your bottom line or to consistently go from losses to profits.

Perhaps a lucid example of what all the fuss is about will drive my point home if you are not already clear about the potential and risks of day trading. Shown below in Figure A.1 is a chart of the E-Mini S&P 500 stock index futures intraday over a three-day period in September 2005. Figure A.2 shows a similar three-day time span in September 2011. Take a few minutes to examine the difference in dollar price range between the two illustrations. Without a doubt the price ranges in 2011 are approximately three times what they were in the year 2000.

FIGURE A.1

E-Mini S&P futures intraday price swings from high to low in September 2005

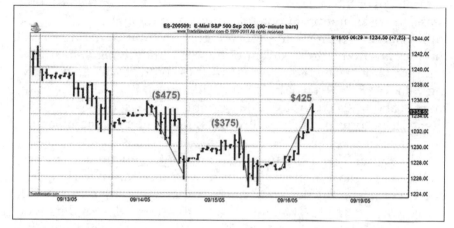

FIGURE A.2

E-Mini S&P futures intraday price swings from high to low in September 2011

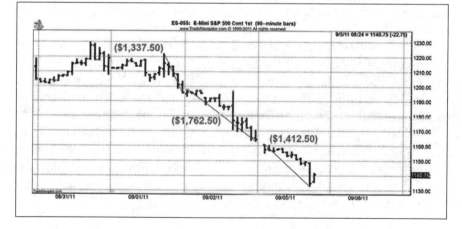

What this essentially means is that futures traders who are willing to put up a margin of from $3,000 to $5,000 per E-Mini S&P futures contract have the profit potential of approximately 40 percent on their money per day. Let us not forget that the other side of the equation is the potential for losing that money as well. While these price swings appear to be rather large, they can be even larger in foreign currency futures trading. On the lower risk and lower potential side, we find stock day trading. Although the price swings have also increased dramatically over the last ten years and even more so over the last three years, the risks and profit potential are considerably less because the initial margin requirement is much higher. In futures trading typical margins are from 1 to 3 percent of the total underlying value of the contract. In other words, a soybean futures contract with an underlying value of \$35,000 can be bought or sold for an initial margin requirement of about \$2,000. In stocks the current margin is 50 percent. In the single stock futures market, with which few traders are familiar, the margin requirement is about 20 percent.

In summary, all the fuss is about the fact, plain and simple, that you can make a great deal of money day trading. That's the good news. The further good news is that there are a number of viable ways to do it. The bad news is that most day traders who are not professionals do not have the tools, the financial ability, the discipline, the procedures, or the organizational skills to make this game work for them.

I believe that my experience, as well as my clearly defined trading methodologies, can help you change your odds to the positive. Yet there is no way that I can guarantee success. The success that any individual can achieve in any field of endeavor is not merely a function of having clear, specific operational procedures but also a function of his own ability to put the rules to work. I have seen some individuals take my tools and use them with great success. On the other hand, I have seen some individuals become marginally successful, while others have continued their losing ways. Why does this happen? Why is it that even though the rules are clear, the procedures are specific, and the methodologies are not subject to interpretation, one individual can achieve success while another fails? The answers to these and even more substantive questions will be found in the chapters that follow.

Jake Bernstein
May 2013
Santa Cruz, California
jake@trade-futures.com
www.jakebernstein.com

CHAPTER 1

What the Day Trading Game Is All About

The day trading game is all about making money. On the surface it would seem that there isn't much more to day trading than making money. To some individuals, however, day trading is more about the challenge and the excitement than it is about the money. Every day our lives present us with many challenges. There are numerous ways in which we can put ourselves in the position of being challenged. Day trading in my view is not something we should do for the challenge. While it is true that a great deal of satisfaction can be gained from being a successful day trader, we must not enter into the day trading game for the purpose of meeting a challenge but rather for the purpose of achieving financial victory.

Given the vast increase in volatility during the 1990s and 2000s, there are more opportunities to profit from large and even small intraday changes now than ever before. At the same time, commissions, computers, and communications costs are also lower than ever before. That combination has created a win-win situation, but only for those who are able to master the game. This, of course, leads to the inevitable question, how do we master the day trading game?

There are literally hundreds of ideas out there in the trading world about how to win as a day trader. A keyword Internet search on the term *day trading* yields 44,800,000 results. That is truly a staggering number; were we to track down every lead, it would leave us no time to actually day trade. And so the good news is that there's a great deal of information out there about day trading. The bad news is that there is so much information, it is impossible to critically assess the accuracy and validity of all of it. Finally, we come to the worst news: I estimate that over 98 percent of the methodologies offered or purported to be successful are neither objective nor profitable.

Today, more than ever before, the aspiring day trader must be especially cautious not to throw away good money on bad methods. Today, more than ever before, the aspiring day trader must be vigilant in doing her homework and research in order to find day trading methods that will make money. While day trading has been presented to—or rather sold to, or rather hyped to—the public as a good thing to do, the fact of the matter is that for most traders, it is a bad thing to do. This is not because day trading is inherently a losing proposition; it is because day trading is not only the most difficult type of trading to execute but also the most difficult at which to succeed.

Day trading is all about taking advantage of large or even small predictable price movements in stocks, Forex, and futures. The day trading game, when played successfully, is about achieving profits using objective, operationally defined, and demonstrably profitable tools. Combined with these tools, a risk management approach is critical for success. But without a profit-maximizing strategy, the day trading game will be all about frustration and losses as opposed to profits and success. It is my intention to share with you in this book several tools that I have developed in order to win the day trading game.

I would like to emphasize the following critically important facts and factors that will facilitate your success as a day trader, whether you use my methods or other effective trading ones.

1. Begin your day trading venture with sufficient capital. By that I mean capital that will not only be purely speculative but also allow you to day trade the markets that interest you with enough money to buffer or withstand a series of losses.

2. Day trade in time frames that are consistent with what you can realistically do. If you intend to sit at the computer all day trading stock index futures using five-minute data for your signals, then make sure you really can be back at the computer every five minutes, or even more frequently, to see if there are new signals.

3. Don't trade too many markets at the same time. Most traders cannot realistically day trade more than several stocks, currencies, or commodities at the same time without either missing signals or making mistakes.

4. Use objective, rule-based entry techniques as opposed to interpretive techniques. To put it another way, don't trade on intuition or "gut feel" because that will not be profitable in the long run, even though initially you may achieve some success. Gut feel is not a trading method or system. Unfortunately, that is the approach most day traders use.

5. Employ strict, risk-based rules for managing your losses. Simply stated, do not assume more risk than your account can tolerate. I will give you some specific time-tested rules for doing so.

6. Use a profit-maximizing strategy that will, if properly implemented, extract the greatest possible profits from winning trades.

7. Be prepared financially and psychologically for a series of losing trades. It is not unusual for day traders to suffer from five to seven consecutive losses.

8. If and when you do suffer a series of consecutive losses, do not take the next profitable trade off your books quickly in order to compensate for the losses. Let your trades run their course by the rules.

9. Use a specific trading model that will help you not only generate your day trades but also determine what to do, when to do it, and how to do it. Having a trading model will also help you identify specific errors you may have made and when you made them.

10. Avoid excessive inputs to your trading strategy; having too much information is just as bad, if not worse, than having too little.

11. It is often better to trade in isolation than it is to surround yourself with news, the opinions of other traders, and a plethora of superfluous input from so-called experts.

In addition to the suggestions cited above, I will share with you in the pages that follow specific trading ideas, methods, and indicators that will give you the edge in day trading.

Finally, no book on day trading, or any type of trading for that matter, would be complete without a clear and concise statement about risk (yes, still another one). I'm certain that you have heard it all before, but I must repeat that day trading involves risk no matter what you may have been told by others. Despite the fact that when you day trade you have no overnight exposure to a loss, there is still exposure during the day. If you believe day trading is easy or that you are virtually guaranteed a profit, you are sadly mistaken. Day trading is at best demanding, time-consuming, and all too often frustrating. Day trading is not an instant cure to financial woes. Day trading is not a game, although many traders consider it to be one. Day trading is a business that, if done correctly and with discipline, can be profitable, but it is by no means easy or a sure thing.

CHAPTER 2

Why Day Trade?

Success as a day trader: it's the American dream. It's the capitalist dream. It's the get-rich-quick dream. It's the entrepreneur's dream. It's the be-your-own-boss-and-work-from-anywhere dream. It's a dream that almost everyone has had at one time or another. But it's also a dream that very few get to pursue and very few get to fulfill. All markets—stock, commodity, and Forex—define volatility. In other words, they move back and forth, often rapidly, all day and all night long. The unstable economic backdrop in the United States and Europe has created an underlying sense of uncertainty that has, in turn, housed itself in a cloak of anxious trading. In order to capitalize on record price movements over small periods of time, professional traders have resorted to such techniques as flash trading, high-frequency trading, so-called dark pools, and algorithmic trading. These highly technical, computerized trading machines buy and sell stocks at a high frequency in large amounts in order to capitalize on small moves that occur during the day. The holding time for these positions is often a matter of seconds, as opposed to hours or days or weeks. It is estimated that some 60 percent of trading in stocks is now characterized by such ultra-short-term forays.

The average investor does not have the financial or technical resources to participate in this fastest of all games. The professional investor has been forced to participate in order to turn a profit in a game that has become highly competitive and highly regulated by government agencies. While professional traders and money managers have moved ahead into high-frequency trading, the day trading game, which was once their domain, has passed on to the average investor. Advances in computer technology, sophisticated software programs for technical analysis, historically low commission costs, and lightning-fast order execution using electronic entry have all combined to make day trading more accessible than ever before. We must not, however, equate accessibility with success. The mere fact that it is easier than ever to day trade does not ipso facto mean that all day traders will be successful. In fact, the reality of day trading can be quite grim. Most day traders are not successful. They have no idea what to do. Most are floundering in a sea of misinformation and disinformation within which it is difficult to obtain and implement strategies that facilitate consistent success.

Although many aspiring day traders see the stock, futures, and Forex markets as their vehicles to financial independence, much of this expectation has been shaped by ongoing promotional campaigns backed by exchanges and brokerage firms. As always, the task that awaits traders and investors is multifaceted:

1. In order to be successful as a day trader, it is critical to understand what day trading is, what it is not, and what to expect from it.

2. Specific trading strategies must be developed in advance in order to identify and isolate potentially profitable opportunities.

3. The markets in which a day trader will trade must be identified. It is not possible to successfully participate in many different markets at one time.

4. A structured procedure must be developed in order to implement objective and organized decisions.

5. Every aspiring and every practicing day trader must know in advance exactly how to determine the appropriate risk level for his account and financial capability. Without knowing the risk for each trade, the end result will most often be loss.

6. Every day trader must define and refine precise procedures to ensure that trades are not being made on the basis of emotion.

Simple as these challenges are to enumerate, they are exceedingly difficult to implement because they require numerous decisions, sufficient starting capital, and highly structured procedures and rules. Without training and education, most traders will not be able to achieve their goals.

Given the multilayered challenges that await and confront all aspiring and practicing day traders, one question naturally arises: why would someone want to day trade? Before we can address the issue of why someone wants to day trade, we need to understand the new definition of day trading. Why do I use the term *new* definition? Most markets now trade at least 20 hours a day continuously, while some are essentially 24-hour markets (e.g., Forex currency trading). Currency futures in Chicago are traded 23 hours a day. Stock index futures trade virtually around the clock. So, before discussing the *why* of day trading, we need to understand the *what* of day trading.

An insomniac can sit in front of her computer and literally trade 24 hours a day, six or even seven days a week. Realistically, this is not possible or palatable for most of us. On the other hand, we can implement day trades during the day session, which is more manageable and does not require attention 24 hours a day. In stocks the day session is clearly defined from the opening to the closing time of the stock market. In the futures markets, many exchanges have differentiated between the day session and the extended session.

For the purposes of this book, I will consider day trading to be *entering and exiting trades during the course of the day session, as defined by the various exchanges or the particular markets or stocks that are being traded.*

Within the context of this definition, there are a number of reasons I can suggest in support of day trading. Note, however, that all of these assume that day trading is approached from an objective standpoint, with specific rules for entry and exit and, moreover, specific rules for limiting losses. Now that we have defined day trading, we can look at some of the reasons for doing it.

REASONS TO DAY TRADE

While the primary reason to day trade is the obvious (mercenary) one—namely, to make money—that goal is unattainable unless other factors are taken care of first.

A viable reason for day trading that might not be obvious to most traders is that the day trader must exit trades by the end of the day. In so doing the day trader is forced not only to take profits but to take losses. Given that most traders blunder by carrying losses too long and exiting profits too quickly, being forced to exit by the end of the day is a great help to the trader who adheres to the requirement that the day trade must be closed out by the end of the day session.

That most obvious reason for day trading is last on my list of importance, and there are two aspects to it. The first part of this reason is, of course, to make a profit. Without a doubt today's volatile markets are conducive to this goal. As an example, I offer Figure 2.1, the Japanese yen futures, showing what can occur on an intraday basis in today's markets. This is not the exception to the rule. Consider also Figure 2.2, which shows the profit potential on an intraday basis in S&P 500 E-Mini futures. Observe that these potential profits all occurred within the course of a day. Remember

FIGURE 2.1

The steep decline in Japanese Yen futures intraday

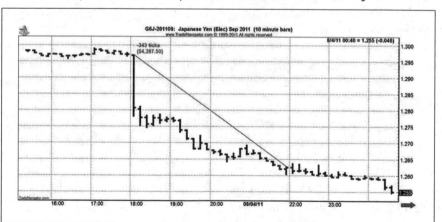

FIGURE 2.2

Intraday moves in S&P futures

also that the profits shown assume that a day trader would have been on the correct side of the market.

The second aspect of this last reason is to maximize your return on capital.

In order to take advantage of these and many more day trading opportunities I will show you how to:

1. Familiarize yourself with how the day trading game is played by professional traders

2. Give you the rules by which you must live as a day trader

3. Show you five day trading methods

4. Tell you how to select your day trades

5. Explain how to manage risk and maximize profits

6. Give you a structured daily procedure to help you focus

ALERTING YOU TO A FEW POTENTIAL PROBLEMS BEFORE THEY HAPPEN

Given the broad scope of day trading, there are many opportunities that present themselves to the day trader. Within the course of the trading day we can implement trades in many different time frames and in many different markets. The possibilities can be, and in many cases prove to be, overwhelming. The newcomer to day trading frequently makes the mistake of either trying to do too much or being afraid and doing too little. Some day traders want to day trade stocks, futures, Forex, and cross currency spread all at the same time. On the other hand, many new day traders are attracted to either the Forex markets or S&P futures. I've heard some new traders say, "My goal is to make $500 per day trading E-Mini S&P futures. Once I have reached my goal, I'm done for the day." To me this means that the trader has arbitrarily decided to limit the profits he can make, which places a top on his potential profits. If there is to be a limit, then the trader should impose that limit on the losing side rather than on the winning one. *There should be no limit to how much a trader wants to make each day.*

Another problem I have seen is in quantity versus quality. The goal of many day traders is to trade as often as possible for relatively small moves. The hope or intention here is to do what has in the past been termed *scalping* but which recently has been given a more politically correct term: *high-frequency trading*. The problem for the average trader is that, although she may make a profit 15 or 20 times in a row for small money, one large loss will consume all of the previous profitable trades, or even exceed them.

The professional high-frequency trader buys and sells positions in a matter of seconds or even fractions of seconds, attempting to achieve large profits using large positions on small price moves. This is a classic issue: would you rather sell a million widgets for a dollar each or five widgets for $200,000 each? *The average day trader cannot achieve success as a high-frequency trader and should not attempt to do so.*

My emphasis is on five quintessential aspects of day trading. Without even one of them, your venture will be either doomed to failure or dependent upon sheer luck; depending on luck is not what successful day traders do.

1. Select trades with a structured trading model.

2. Follow through using specific trigger tools.

3. Maximize profit strategies using a clear and organized procedure.

4. Utilize a specific stop-loss procedure combined with risk evaluation prior to entering a trade.

5. Set up organizational procedures.

My emphasis is on structure, clearly defined trading triggers, clarity, and profit-maximizing strategies. The procedures I will illustrate can be used on a daily basis within the context of my methods, and I will further emphasize the importance of being a specialist rather than a generalist. In other words, you will focus rather than be scattered in your methods, markets, and time frames.

I recently received a phone call from a new mentoring student. It was clear that he needed considerable assistance:

"Good morning, Jake. The market today has me very confused. My 5-minute S&P chart indicates the start of the new uptrend. On the other hand, my 15-minute chart is still heading down and my 30-minute chart remains in an uptrend that has been with us for over a week now. I found this confusing, so I also looked at my 90-minute chart, after which I consulted my daily chart to see if there were new indicators and triggers there. I examined my weekly chart to see if the seasonal trend was on course and verified that with the long-term cycle on my monthly chart. I then returned to my intraday chart and observed that my 1-minute chart had just given a buy signal, and that confused me even more. I don't know what to do. Do you have any suggestions?"

My answer? "Focus on one time frame, focus on one method, trade within the time frame that initiated your trade, do not consult any other methods or systems, and don't complicate the issue with superfluous information that has nothing to do with the day trade."

That is also my best advice to you. Keep it simple. Keep it clear. Keep it organized. The method that gets you in will in most cases be the method that gets you out. The method that gets you in stands on its own. The procedures you have established ahead of time are the ones you will follow. The one exception to this rule is market exit. *While our market entries for day trading can and will be completely objective, by virtue of the necessity to exit trades at the end of each day, some of our exits may not be as objective, but we will have procedures for our exit strategy.*

CHAPTER 3

How to Do It, Part I

Theories and opinions about profitable day trading methods and procedures abound. If you have not yet discovered that almost every trader has his favorite procedure and method, you will certainly find that out sooner rather than later. In some ways that's a good thing; it creates a great diversity of opinion as well as a great diversity of positions. That helps to create a two-sided market, rather than one in which most traders are thinking and acting the same way most of the time. But you will also discover, if you have not already done so, that a vast portion of what transpires in the real world of day trading has nothing to do with clear and objective procedures but rather is the result of gut feel. That's not for us!

To achieve a clear understanding of day trading procedures and methods, it is important to first understand the big-picture trading structure, or what I call the STF (setup, trigger, and follow through). Figure 3.1 shows my STF trading model, which will help you understand and organize the overall structure of a trade. When you understand a trade's structure, you will also understand the differences between timing triggers, timing signals, methods of analysis, trading tools, trading systems, and trading methods.

In Chapter 2 I referred to high-frequency trading, which is very profitable. Some of the firms involved in high-frequency trading have amassed huge sums of money. How do they do it?

FIGURE 3.1

The STF trading model

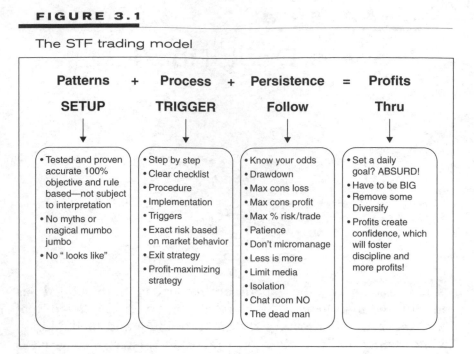

The answer is simple: by computer. Computers evaluate a variety of rules or algorithms, combining them with perfectly legitimate information purchased from the exchanges regarding where different types of orders are located. This information is combined in a trading rule–based approach; the computers automatically place entry and exit orders for large positions, seeking to take advantage of very small but predictable price moves. And they do quite well at it. You may ask why we can't do the same thing. We could if we had the resources to pay for the technology—both hardware and software—and for the information that runs the engine of the program. But even when they have access to clearly objective rules and procedures, most traders fail to apply them consistently for a variety of reasons.

Although the computer clearly has the edge, such information would be useless unless applied consistently as part of a trading formula or procedure. The procedure begins with a trading model: a specific construct or concept that explains how the various moving parts of the trading procedure are interrelated and connected. A trading model provides a consistent structure and procedure for every trade and every trading decision. This seemingly complex if-then scenario forms the basis of the trading approach. I say seemingly complex because it is much less complicated than you might think.

Although it need not be complicated, we need to have a specific model upon which our trading is based. If you have that specific structure, you are immediately way ahead of most day traders. If you understand what a trading model is, you are more likely to realize its value and more likely to use one. You may be familiar with such market concepts as the Elliott wave or Fibonacci-based rules. You may also be familiar with the seasonal approach to trading. These are all examples of trading concepts, but they are not trading models.

In the hierarchy of trading the model comes second. At the peak of the hierarchy is the trading structure. Every potentially profitable trading model I'm aware of adheres to a trading structure. I believe there is only one solid trading structure, and I will discuss that later. First, however, let's take a look at a few trading models.

1. If a stock is moving higher based on set, clear, and objective criteria, buy if the price of the stock declines to its 18-day moving average and exit the position if it is not profitable within 4 days after entry. Take your profit or reduce your exposure if and when the stock achieves a 5 percent target from your entry price.

2. Buy 30-year Treasury bond futures on the second to last business day of each month, and exit the position win or lose by the end of the second trading day of the new month.

In each of the above cases the model tells us when to get in, when to get out, and when to take a profit or loss. These models are very specific. They contain all of the information a trader needs in order to make a decision. They are missing one important element, though: they do not give us a clear enough idea of how much risk may be involved in implementing these rules. The good news about these trading models is that they are rule-based. The bad news is that they are not sufficiently specific. But they have one overriding similarity: they are structured.

Each of the hypothetical examples above contain the basic concept of setup, trigger, and follow through, though they do so in relatively vague terms. In order to best understand the day trading methods and procedures in this book, I urge you to spend some time studying and fully understanding the STF trading model. Whether you decide to implement some of my suggested methods, those you learn elsewhere, or your own, I believe the STF model will be very helpful to you. Because it is highly organized, completely objective, and rule based, it will help you know what to do, when and if to do it, how to manage the risk, and how to maximize the profit.

SETUP

The setup portion of the trading model requires us to use a particular pattern or patterns that have shown themselves to be reliable or predictable over time. There are many patterns traders use in their efforts to make money. The traditional patterns, including trend lines, head and shoulders formations, flags, pennants, support, and resistance, with few exceptions have not been sufficiently researched. Although I'm sure I will ruffle some feathers when I say this, I do not find such popular methods as Fibonacci, Elliott wave, Gann, or other market geometry approaches to trading to be useful or profitable. Having said that, I give credit to anyone who can use those methods profitably on a consistent basis. These methods are more judgment based than rule based.

A setup is a pattern or repetitive relationship that can be back tested for accuracy and results, whether actual or hypothetical. A setup can be operationally defined as an algorithm or a specific 100-percent-objective rule. Although there are literally hundreds of patterns that traders look at, the fact is that a relatively small number of them can be objectively defined and tested.

Perhaps an example will clarify what I mean by a setup.

Figure 3.2 shows a seasonal futures chart of MMM Minnesota Mining and Manufacturing Company from 1970 through 2010. At the top of the chart I show the normalized weekly trend for the stock during this period of time. At the bottom of the chart I show the weeks and months, along with readings that indicate the percentage of time the stock has ended each week higher or lower than the previous week. I have highlighted the periods of highest

FIGURE 3.2

The weekly seasonal stock chart for MMM, showing the
normalized trend

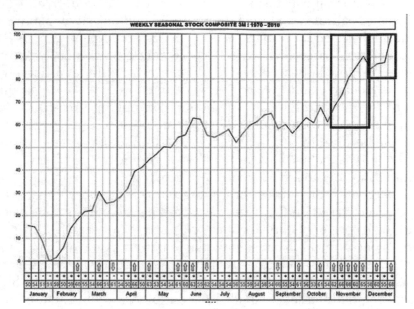

probability up moves with boxes. These are time frames that denote
the most reliable series of weeks for higher prices. We know that
these periods of time tend to bring higher prices because the percentage readings at the bottom of the chart indicate an up movement.

As you can see from the readings for the month of November,
the percentages are all at 60 percent or higher, with an arrow pointing up. This is a statistical fact, based on the real historical behavior of this stock during the month of November and throughout
the year. This is not an assumption or an interpretation. Obviously MMM has not moved higher 100 percent of the time during
November, but the probabilities are significant based on the historical behavior of this stock over the course of many years. Compare
this information with what you may have learned or what you
may be using in terms of statistical fact as opposed to mythology
or conjecture.

The chart also shows a period of up movement from late May into mid-June. While it could be argued with good reason that the time span of data history for this stock is not sufficient to reach a solid historical conclusion, the facts that we have derived from this historical study are much more useful and objective than what is normally used by traders. Data on stock and commodity prices are available to those who wish to perform such research. Whether one is seeking daily, weekly, monthly, or even intraday prices, the data is available and tests can be performed in order to determine the historical validity of any method or concept one intends to use. Remember that we are not looking for patterns that are 100 percent reliable because they don't exist. If we do find such patterns, the probability is that we have not looked at a sufficient number of repetitions in order to form a good statistical test.

Arguably, the process of finding patterns is subject to several limitations based on the way in which the searches are conducted and the length of historical data being used in our search. This pattern is one of many. That some reliable patterns do exist is a testament to the fact that there is order and predictability in the markets. This flies in the face of the so-called random walk theory, which purports that market behavior is a random event and that efforts at predicting market trends or prices are useless. This topic is grist for the mill of academics and not relevant to our purposes. The primary reason for my mentioning it is to show that our procedure begins with a setup and goes much further when we understand that any setup is not 100-percent predictable and therefore requires that we move on to the next step, a trigger.

Trigger

Every good setup requires a good trigger. Most traders use the term *timing indicator* to denote a particular technical signal for buying or selling. In my trading model, a timing trigger without a pattern to support it results in poor accuracy. In other words the setup must be used in conjunction with the trigger. If a particular setup suggests that a trade should be entered into either long or short, I must wait for the setup to trigger entry. Some traders use the term *confirm* or *confirmation* to denote a trigger. The setup example in Figure 3.2 requires a trigger in order to increase its accuracy. The fact that this particular stock tends to move higher over 60 percent of the time in November is not sufficient unless I'm willing to settle for that kind of accuracy. My goal is to increase accuracy to the highest level possible for the obvious purpose of making a profit. The trigger tool allows me to take a valid setup, validate the setup with a trigger, and then go on to the next step.

A setup or pattern to buy a particular market must be accompanied by a trigger to buy. Conversely a sell setup must be accompanied by a trigger to sell. As in the case of setups, there are numerous triggers. Many traders fail to understand that most triggers or timing indicators in use today are based on price and therefore simply reflect what the underlying price trend may be. Traditional triggers or timing tools such as moving averages when used according to the standard rules tend to be very low in accuracy. This fact is easily demonstrated statistically. The sad and unfortunate truth about moving averages used in the traditional way—moving averages of closing prices—is that accuracy is frequently less than 30 percent. In the long run, many moving-average-based systems make money. That's the good news. The bad news is that on the road to making money in these systems, traders tend to suffer numerous consecutive losses and a serious depletion of capital. Unless you are using a moving-average-based system that incorporates rules and features distinctly different from those generally available to traders, I urge you to avoid them because you may be very disappointed in the results.

As an example of how a trigger works let's again refer to MMM, selecting the month of November as the setup. This means that as I enter the month of November, I will need to trigger the setup. Given that the setup is to buy the stock at some point in November, most likely early in the month, I will begin looking for a buy timing trigger to get me into the stock based on the setup shown in Figure 3.2.

One of the timing triggers I use in my work is the momentum indicator. Without explaining momentum at this juncture, I will examine how momentum triggers entry on the buy side during the period of optimum up movement based on what the setup has previously told us. Figure 3.3 shows the MMM chart with momentum at the bottom of the chart. My timing rule states that in order for a buy setup to be triggered, momentum must be a

FIGURE 3.3

MMM momentum buy trigger during a period of historical seasonal up movement

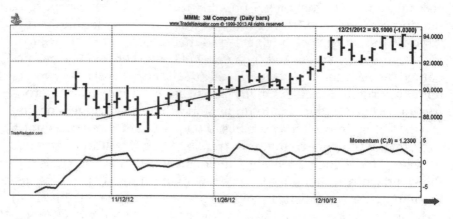

positive number when the optimum time frame for higher prices is entered. The chart for MMM tells us that historically this occurs in late October or early November. Accordingly, I go to the MMM chart and begin looking for a trigger to enter the buy side based on what the setup has told us.

FOLLOW THROUGH

The third part of my trading model is follow through, a term that may immediately conjure up the idea that this part of the strategy consists only of maximizing profits. That is not the case. Follow through consists of two parts. The first is managing the risk, commonly known as the stop loss, and the second is the profit-maximizing strategy.

Most day traders make the mistake of grabbing numerous quick, small profits and taking fewer slower, large losses. At the end of the day (no pun intended), their percentage of winning trades may be considerably higher than their percentage of losing trades, but the sum total of losses frequently exceeds the sum total of profits. This is a classic example of how accuracy as a percent may be illusory. Accuracy is important, of course, but having a larger average winning trade compared to an average losing trade is more important. The only way in which day traders, or for that matter any traders or investors, can emerge victorious in this game is to have a profit-maximizing strategy that will give them large, winning trades.

The profit-maximizing strategy for each of the methods I discuss in this book is slightly different. I like to trade in units of three: three contracts in futures, six contracts, nine contracts, etc., or, in stocks, 300 shares, 600 shares, 900 shares, and so on. I do this in order to exit my position in a way that quickly minimizes or even eliminates risk while at the same time allowing the flexibility to maximize profits. The core aspect of my trading model consists of two central themes: the danger zone and the final one-third trailing stop strategy.

The Danger Zone

I define the danger zone as the period of time from which a trade is entered up to the time the trade reaches its first objective. The first objective or profit target for any given trade is a function of the underlying method that gets us into that trade. The goals of having a first profit target are to take some money off the table as well as to provide the opportunity to reduce exposure to a loss to effectively zero. Before getting into a trade we want to know our risk of loss and our exact profit target. By placing an order to exit our trade for part of the position at the first profit target, we are able, in many cases, to exit a portion of the trade at a profit while managing the remaining two-thirds of the trade to lock in more profit while essentially eliminating risk.

PROFIT-MAXIMIZING STRATEGY

In the investing and trading business it has often been jokingly said that the definition of an investment is "a day trade that ended the day at a loss." While this may be humorous to those who have never day traded, it is nonetheless sad but true. Many day traders allow their losses to run, failing to exit losing trades by the end of the day. By definition a day trade is a trade that is closed out at the end of the day. Whether you define a day as 23 hours (the trading day length for currency futures) or a much shorter day or stocks, the fact is that a day trade is closed out by the end of the session. Unfortunately, some unskilled and undisciplined traders refuse to take their losses at the end of the day and usually incur a much worse loss at some point in the future.

On the other hand, taking a quick profit on a day trade may not be the solution either. In order to compensate for losses that are part of the trading game, your profits on winning trades need to be as large as possible. That old saying that 80 percent of your money is going to be made in 20 percent of your trades is apropos in day trading as well as in longer-term trading.

ADVANTAGES OF THE STF TRADING MODEL

If I could teach you only one thing in this book, it would be the setup, trigger, and follow through trading model. I believe that if you understand and master the concepts and applications of the STF trading model, you will be way ahead of most other day traders. Internalizing the concepts of STF and applying them as part of every single day trade you make will spell the difference between profits and losses, success and failure, understanding and frustration. Because I believe that the difference between winning and losing traders is significantly related to the use of their trading model, I conclude this chapter with a list of benefits to be derived from the use of STF, no matter what trading and timing methods you use:

1. The STF model will help you be organized. If you are organized, you will make system-related trades as opposed to ones that are prompted by emotions.

2. If you make a mistake somewhere in the sequence of your trading decision and your process is based on the STF model, it will be easier for you to discover where or when you made your mistake and fix it more quickly.

3. The STF model, if used as a screening tool for all trades, will keep you out of trades that do not conform to fully operational and completely objective criteria.

4. Because profit-maximizing strategies are required in order to achieve large profits, using STF will help you be more profitable.

5. If you use the STF model consistently you will avoid trading based on rumors, intuition, tips, emotions, or other non-system-related inputs. This alone will save you considerable money as well as frustration.

6. Finally, using the STF model you will see your results as they relate to your behaviors. You will always know what you did and why you did it. Far too many traders don't know why they lost money on a given trade, so their loss is not a learning experience.

The STF model will not only allow you to implement a concise and objective trading plan, it will also give you an opportunity to determine where you may have gone wrong in the event that you take a loss that is not part of the trading system. This goes back to what I called earlier the smart loss and the stupid loss. The STF model will serve as your guide in minimizing the stupid loss, maximizing the profit, and giving you the structure you need to increase your accuracy while at the same time maximizing your bottom-line profits.

CHAPTER 4

How to Do It, Part II

Now we will jump right into the reality of day trading, using specific trading methods as they relate to the setup, trigger, and follow through (STF) trading structure. If you have read any of my other books about day trading or attended the any of my seminars or webinars, you may already be familiar with the gap trading method. I begin with this approach because it not only is one of the least time-consuming ways of day trading but also enjoys relatively high accuracy in addition to its ease of application.

TRADING WITH GAPS

Some people believe that in order to be a successful day trader you need to sit in front of the computer all day long watching numbers changing and screens blinking with news blaring in the background, nonstop information coming in over the telephone and radio, and/or constant order entry and exit. While some of this stereotypical characterization of day trading may be accurate, the fact is that such time and attention is only necessary if you plan to trade many times each day. Note, however, that the sheer volume of day trades you complete is in no way positively correlated with the amount of money you make. In this case, less is usually more.

I will assume you have already acquired or implemented the necessary equipment and/or procedures to play the game. If you plan to actively trade using the methods presented herein, you will, of course, need a trading account. Another necessary tool is your computer, along with a suitable charting software program that will allow you to use the indicators and tools presented in this book. At this point, however, I want to stress the importance of having real-time price data (as opposed to delayed data) for all day trade methods taught in this book. Some newcomers to day trading erroneously believe they can day trade profitably using data that is anywhere from 10 to 30 minutes late. While this procedure may save you money on data, you cannot be a profitable day trader using delayed data. Just don't do it! Why attempt to win at the most difficult game in the financial markets with a handicap? Spend the extra money for live, real-time, streaming data, and give yourself the best possible chance to win. Without clear and correct knowledge of prices, you may very well miss trades, enter or exit trades late, or take unnecessary losses as you "zig" while the markets are "zagging."

Some aspiring day traders believe they can use free online trading software for their charts and indicators. This is usually not advisable either. Some brokerage firms will offer you free software as part of the account you open with them. Some of these programs will work with my methods and some won't. Check the features of your software, whether free or not, to make sure you can get the indicators and studies you will need. It is critical that you have the right tools for the job. Day trading on the cheap is not a good idea.

WHY USE GAPS?

As I stated at the beginning of the chapter, this is not the first time I have written about trading with gaps. This method has appeared in a number of my other books. Some of you may already be using a gap trading method and may therefore be familiar with the rules and procedures. This chapter offers more detailed information on trading with gaps as well as a review of what has been presented previously (you can visit my website www.trade-futures.com for examples of my day trading methods). This review, as well as specific rules and examples combined with new material, will help solidify your learning.

Let's begin with the definition of a gap within the context of our STF trading model.

Defining a Gap

A gap trade is set up when a stock or commodity opens for the trading day above the last daily price high or below the last daily price low. A gap up occurs when the opening price is greater than the high of the previous day and a gap down occurs when the opening price is below the low of the previous day. A gap down setup is the first part of a buy pattern, whereas a gap up opening is the setup for a sell trigger.

It is relatively easy to recognize a gap up or down opening visually by looking at the chart or electronically by allowing your computer to scan stocks or futures after they have opened to find those that have opened with these gaps. On any given day there can be hundreds of gap openings up or down across all markets. *It is therefore very important to be selective about the stocks or commodities you trade with gaps, which can be accomplished by using a filter for selecting gaps.*

I have found that traders are more inclined to use gaps in their trading if they understand what causes opening gaps to occur. There are numerous possible causes, but the overriding one is emotionally based buying or selling due to underlying fundamentals. Very positive news about a stock usually results in a gap higher opening, while very negative news usually results in a gap lower opening.

Here is a list of some of the reasons for gap openings as well as some characteristics of gap openings. To further your understanding, I've included some details on what opening gaps tend to indicate or predict:

- Bullish news causes gap up openings.
- Bearish news causes gap down openings.
- A gap can be the start of something big or something small that is very accurate.
- Some of the largest one-day moves in history have been gap days.
- Gaps are caused by emotional responses to news; emotional responses are often wrong.
- Professionals take advantage of emotional reactions to news.
- Gaps aren't necessarily related to underlying trends.
- Some of the most profitable gap down openings have developed in underlying bull markets.

- Some of the most profitable gap up openings have developed in underlying bear markets.
- Gap days tend to produce large trading ranges.
- Gap days tend to be pivotal; many important tops and bottoms occur on gap days in stocks and futures.
- Gap days can be high trading volume days.

LOOKING AT SOME GAPS

The schematic of a gap lower opening is shown in Figure 4.1.
A gap higher opening is shown in Figure 4.2.

FIGURE 4.1

A gap lower opening

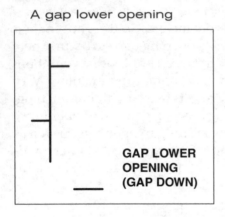

FIGURE 4.2

A gap higher opening

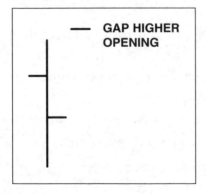

FIGURE 4.3

A gap by trade

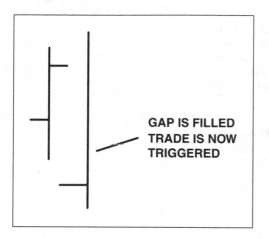

**GAP IS FILLED
TRADE IS NOW
TRIGGERED**

Within the framework of the STF trading model, a gap lower opening is a buy setup, while a gap higher opening is a sell setup. Exit is either at a stop loss, at a target, and/or at the end of the day. A gap trade can also be exited the next day, but then it no longer qualifies as a valid gap trade. As you can see, it is not merely an opening above the previous daily high or below the previous daily low that signals a gap trade entry; there must be a penetration back into the range of the previous day. *Without a trigger, a gap setup is not a call to action!* Figures 4.3 to 4.5 illustrate additional aspects and rules for the gap trade schematically.

Gap Lower Open is a BUY SETUP that is Triggered when the LOW of a Previous Day is Penetrated

A gap by trade is triggered after a lower opening and penetration back into the previous day's trading range. In other words, the market comes back up into the range of the previous day, thereby triggering a buy.

FIGURE 4.4

A gap buy trade triggered and closed out by the end of the day

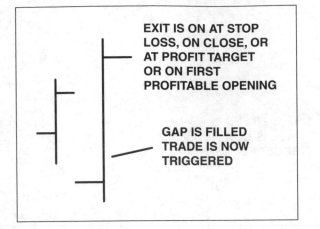

EXIT IS ON AT STOP
LOSS, ON CLOSE, OR
AT PROFIT TARGET
OR ON FIRST
PROFITABLE OPENING

GAP IS FILLED
TRADE IS NOW
TRIGGERED

FIGURE 4.5

A gap buy trade triggered and closed out on first profitable opening

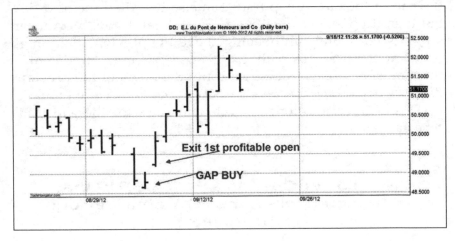

FIGURE 4.6

Opening gap size

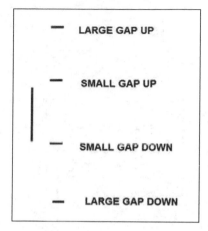

EXAMPLES AND ILLUSTRATIONS

Now that we have looked at some of the ideal variations on the theme of the gap buy and sell trades, let's turn to some actual examples within the context of STF. Remember that a setup occurs when a market opens gap higher or gap lower, the trigger occurs when there is a penetration back into the previous day's range, and the follow through consists of several exit strategies, one of which is a stop loss and the others profit-maximizing procedures.

Figure 4.7 illustrates five gap trades in Xerox (XRX) stock, four of which triggered. The third gap from the left is the one that did not trigger.

As you can see in Figure 4.8 not all gaps trigger. Remember the STF model. If there is no trigger, there is no trade. Do not make the mistake that so many day traders do when it comes to gap trades. They will trade them whether there is a trigger or not. *This significantly decreases the accuracy of the gap trade and is not part of the trading method.*

FIGURE 4.7

Gap trades in XRX

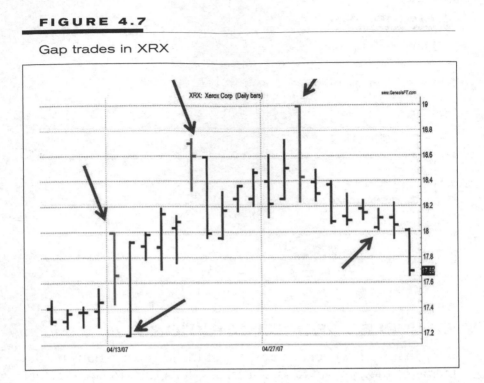

Figure 4.9 illustrates a few more gap trades. I have marked gap openings, but note again that not all gaps trigger. Some stocks during certain periods of time will have more gaps than others. In and of itself, this does not mean anything. Your job as a day trader is to identify opening gaps and to trade them according to the STF method and rules.

Having said that, remember my previous statement that there are many possible gaps each day. We can reduce the number of markets we need to follow by using a filter or a scan, which will eliminate certain types of stocks. For example, you may want to eliminate gap trades that occur in very low-priced stocks or in stocks that trade very low volume. I suggest that your gap trading should be limited to stocks that trade greater than $5 per share that also have had an average daily trading volume of at least 1 million shares for the past 10 days. If you find that your list of potential candidates is still too large, you can increase the volume requirement to 5 million shares on average for the past 10 days, or you can

[handwritten notes at top:]

6:30 - 1:00 =

13 - 6.5 = 6.5 hours

6.5 hours × 60 m/hr

= 390 Minutes ≥ 39 Min/stock

FIGURE 4.8

A few gaps up and down in SBUX. Not all gaps trigger. Of the four here, only one triggered. Do note, however, that the one gap that did trigger was very profitable.

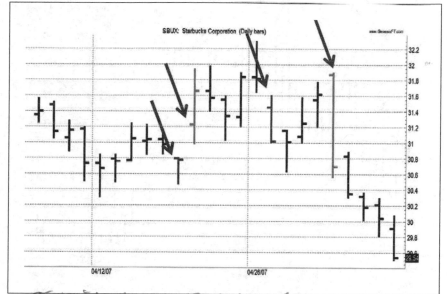

[handwritten notes below chart:]

1st stock is 19.5 Min after open
Last is 19.5 Min before close

go even higher. You can also change the price range within which you search for gaps to reduce the number of possible trades. Quality is more important than quantity!

Let's look at a few more gap trade examples. Figure 4.10 shows gap trades in one of my favorite gap trade stocks, Archer Daniels Midland (ADM). As you can see, the gaps tend to be frequent, and the follow through tends to be large.

Figure 4.11 shows ADM gap trades in 2011, four years after the 2007 chart shown in Figure 4.10. As you can see, ADM is still a "gappy" stock.

Gaps in 24-hour Markets

Gap trading in 24-hour markets poses a special case because there is often no time between the close of one day and the opening of the next. Most gap trades in currency futures—fur, for example—will

FIGURE 4.9

Gaps in DELL

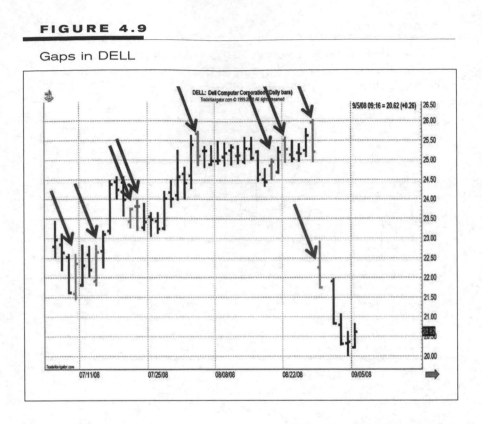

occur from Friday to Monday because the markets close on what is Friday afternoon and then open again on Sunday evening in the United States.

The gap will occur on a Sunday opening.

So-called 23-hour trading has resulted in fewer gaps in currency futures, but the ones that do occur tend to get filled more frequently and to be fairly large in their outcome. This chart shows only two gaps in the Japanese yen, of which only one was filled. The outcome was very profitable.

The Importance of Large Range Days

Unless you can maintain near-perfect accuracy in your day trades, you must depend on large moves to make the bottom line difference for you. In the final analysis, you will find that most day trades will balance off, while the large moves will give you your net profits.

FIGURE 4.10

Gaps in ADM, 2007

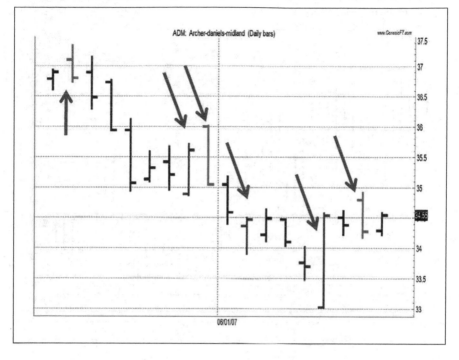

FIGURE 4.11

Gap trades in ADM, 2011

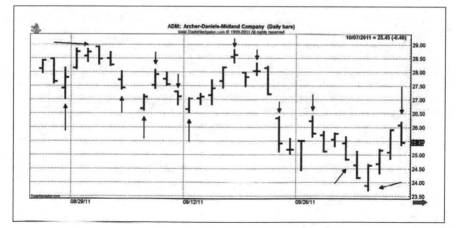

FIGURE 4.12

Gap trades in Japanese yen futures: 23-hour trading—fewer gaps but better ones

FIGURE 4.13

Gap trades that triggered in Aussie dollar Euro currency Forex pair

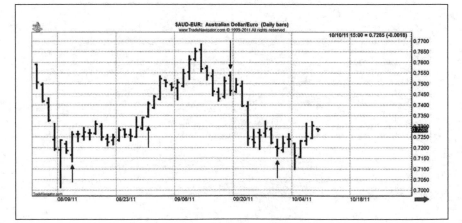

FIGURE 4.14

Large-range gap days make the bottom-line difference.

In other words, if your experience is at all comparable to mine, you will have numerous small winners and numerous small losers that will effectively balance each other out. The big winners are, therefore, the ones that will make all the difference. You cannot get the big winners unless you have a profit-maximizing strategy.

Most day traders will take profits on the fast, small moves and ultimately leave a considerable amount of potential profit on the table. The large moves will make all the difference. As an example, see Figure 4.14.

Exit strategies designed to maximize profits are critical to success as a day trader. As you progress in your day trading career, you will find that profit-maximizing strategies are critical no matter what trading method you are using.

EXIT STRATEGIES FOR LONG GAP TRADE

Now let's take a look at a few exit strategies designed to maximize profits.

Exit at Stop Loss

Once a gap trade has been filled, your stop loss should be placed below the low of the day at the time the gap trade was entered. Let's say that the low on a stock yesterday was 28.80. Today the stock opened at 28.60 or, in other words, the gap lower opening. The stock then begins to move up. Because you have placed your buy stop order at 28.64, your order to buy is triggered and you are now long the stock. You can place your initial stop loss now below the 28.60 level, at 28.50, for example.

As you progress with your gap trading you will realize that on occasion after a gap trade has been triggered for entry into a return to its low of the day for gap by trade or its high of the day for gap short trade, you must allow sufficient room for that stock or commodity to test its high or low of the day. That means you must avoid doing what most people do, which is to place your stop loss one or two cents above or below the high of the day or, in commodities, one or two ticks below the high or low of the day. In other words, you must give your trade some room to trigger an entry and then "test" or revisit its low or high of the day.

A good rule of thumb for placing your stop loss is to allow about 10 percent of the daily trading range as your stop. In the example cited above, if the trading range at the time the buy stop was triggered was $.45, you would allow 4.5 cents, rounded to 5 cents, for the stop loss. Finally, remember it is very important to get out of the danger zone, meaning that you need a first target. A good first target is 50 percent of the range of the day before.

Exit at Profit Target

I suggest using 50 percent of the previous day's trading range as your first target and 100 percent of the previous day's trading range as your second target. For example, let's say that on the previous day the trading range was 35 as the high of the day and 31 as the low. The range is therefore four cents. The first target would be the exact midpoint of the previous day's trading range and the second target would be the high of the previous day in the case of a buy trigger would be. If you trade in units of three—for example, 300 shares—your third position would carry a trailing stop loss, and, if not stopped out, exit would be at the end of the day or market on close. On occasion you may want to hold a day trade through to the next profitable opening in order to maximize profit, which can be a risky proposition.

Exit on First Profitable Opening

First profitable opening (FPO) is defined as the first opening subsequent to your entry that shows you a profit as calculated from your entry, no matter how large or small that profit may be. Trading methods and systems that use FPO exit tend to be very high in accuracy, provided that their underlying trigger is accurate. If you decide to hold your last gap day trade position for the first profitable opening, you need to protect your position breakeven stop loss. In practice this is a risky proposition; the trade may open beyond your stop, in which case the breakeven stop would not protect you from turning a profitable trade into a losing one.

FIGURE 4.15

Apple gap trade with exit FPO

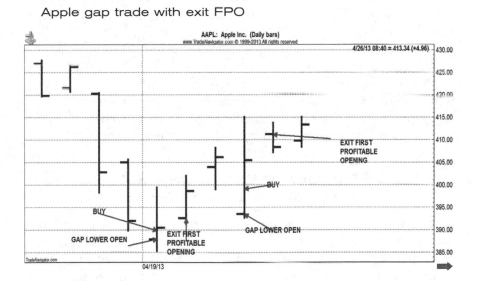

COMBINED STRATEGY ON MULTIPLE CONTACTS

As I've said, I prefer to trade in multiples of three. In futures this would mean three contracts, or in stocks it would mean 300 shares unless, of course, you trade 100 shares and divide your lot into three units of 33 shares. The idea is to establish your position in a way that will allow you to exit part of your position at different targets, as discussed earlier. In stocks this means you will pay an extra commission each time you liquidate your partial position, but I believe that what you gain in flexibility and profits will more than compensate for the additional commissions. Let's elaborate on the procedures for exiting a gap trade.

Exit One at Profit Target One and Raise Stop to Break Even

Profit target one for a gap trade is 50 percent of the range of the previous day. At this point you liquidate a third of your position, place a trailing stop on another third, locking in 75 percent of the profit, and place a stop at breakeven on the last position. Breakeven is defined as the original trigger price. Please note the difference between the original entry price and the original trigger price. If you have entered a buy stop order at 2880, your order becomes a market order as soon as 2880 is hit. That means you could be filled at 2880, 2881, 2882, 2883, 2884, etc., depending upon how fast the stock is moving and what the other resting orders might be. For the purpose of consistency, I prefer to do all calculations based on what the official trigger price would be, as opposed to the actual entry price. This way if you contact me about a particular trade, we are using standardized entry and exit points.

Exit One at End of Day and One at Profit Target Two

After having exited one position at the first target and getting out of the danger zone by trailing stops on remaining positions, you can liquidate another position at the end of the day. You may also exit your second position at profit target, which is the entire range of the previous day.

GAP TRIGGER VARIABLES

While the underlying concept of the gap trade makes good sense and has face validity, there is more there than meets the eye. Simply opening below the low or above the high of the previous day actually oversimplifies the concept. There are other variables that can be considered in executing a gap trade. This makes the gap trade fertile ground for those who wish to do their own research. Consider the following gap variables:

1. Size of gap in cents or ticks: Not all gap openings are the same size; the bigger the gap, the better the trade. A stock may open ten cents or two dollars below its previous day's low. I have found that the larger the opening gap size, the more likely the trade is to be profitable if it triggers. The larger the gap, however, the less likely it will be to trigger; therefore you must consider this variable in selecting the gap trades you want to enter.

2. The size of penetration into the previous daily range: Is a two-cent penetration back into the previous day's range better than a five-cent one? My research has found that a percentage of the previous day's range may be the best solution to this dilemma. If we use a penetration that is too small—for example, one cent in stocks or one tick in futures—we may not be allowing sufficient room for a valid trigger. On the other hand, if we take too large a penetration size, we may give up too much of the potential profit. As a day trader you must strike the proper balance.

3. Size of stop loss: We know from the considerable back testing that larger stops tend to get better results. I have recommended a stop loss that is 10 percent of the range of the previous day.

4. Initial profit target: Review the suggestions for profit target given earlier.

Size of Trigger

Let's take a look at several gap trades in stocks and futures.

FIGURE 4.16

Size of trigger

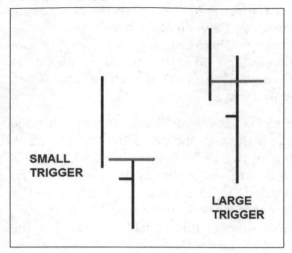

FIGURE 4.17

Gap buys

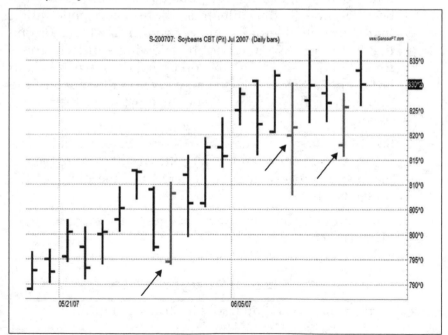

FIGURE 4.18

Gap buy and exit

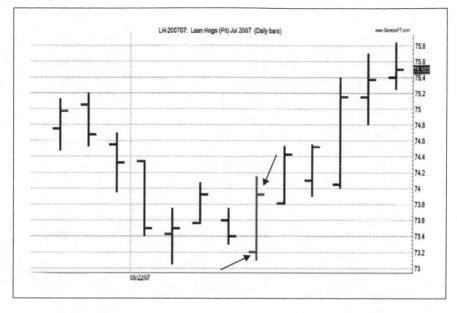

FIGURE 4.19

Gap down not filled—no trade

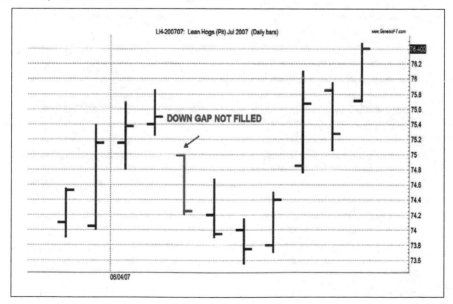

FIGURE 4.20

Gap filled—buy trade

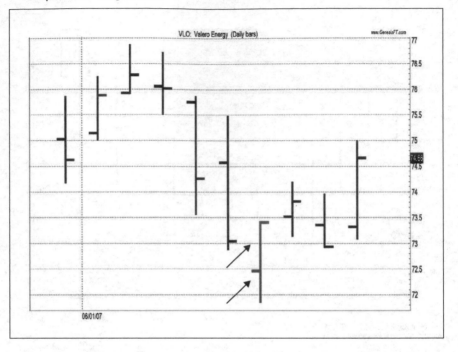

FIGURE 4.21

Buy gaps and profit targets

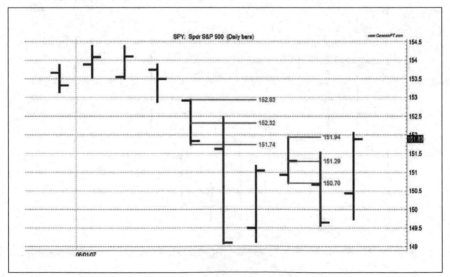

CHAPTER 5

How to Do It, Part III

Many different price relationships can occur in the markets. Many traders only look at the closing price of the market. In so doing they fail to understand the importance of closing prices in relation to the daily high, low, or opening price. Given price metrics to look at each day, it behooves a day trader to consider the various possibilities and how they may be used as either timing triggers or as tools by which to project market direction. My work over the last four decades has led me to the conclusion that, in terms of their predictive validity, some of the most important price relationships are those between the opening and closing prices on any given day.

TRIGGER 3: OPEN VERSUS CLOSE

When the closing price of a stock or commodity market on any given day is higher than the opening price, the probability is that demand for shares or contracts is higher than the supply; this is a bullish indication. When the closing price of a stock or commodity market on any given day is lower than the opening price, the probability is that supply of shares or contracts is higher than demand, a bearish indication.

In an uptrend the probability on any given day is that the close will be higher than the open; in a downtrend the probability on any given day is that the close will be lower than the open.

FIGURE 5.1

Close greater than open 83 percent of the time in uptrend.
In a market that is trending higher, the closing price of each
bar is often higher than the opening price of each bar.

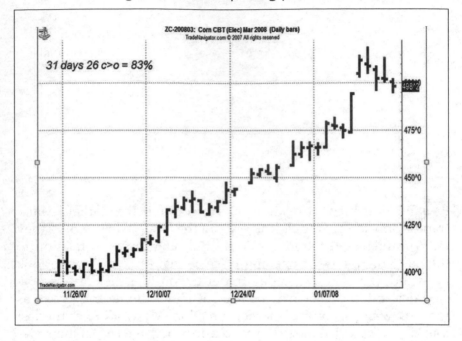

This can be easily demonstrated by looking at several charts in
Figures 5.1 and 5.2.

Although the relationship between the opening and closing price will not always be as obvious as it is in these examples,
we can represent them in a simpler and more operational fashion
by using moving averages (MA) as indications of trend changes.
Note that this method, which I called the 8OC, (buying or selling
based on crossovers of closing prices) is distinctly different than
the popular use of moving averages. As you know, most moving
average–based systems compare two moving averages of closing
prices or three moving averages of closing prices, and make decisions on crossovers of the averages. Such traditional applications
of moving average–based systems tend to have very low inaccu-
racy, very large drawdown, and frequently do poorly in sideways
markets. Furthermore such systems tend to miss entries near tops

FIGURE 5.2

Close less than open 74 percent of the time in downtrend.
In a market that is trending lower, the closing price of each
bar is often lower than the opening price of each bar.

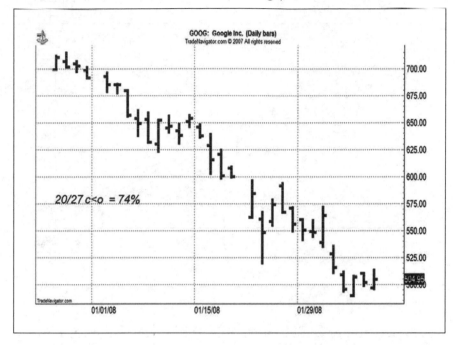

and bottoms, frequently getting in and getting out late. I believe
the 8OC method, as I have developed and designed it, overcomes
many of the shortcomings typical in traditional moving average–
based systems. I do not suggest that the 8OC is in any way a day
trader's panacea; however, I do believe it is exceptionally useful
and capable of capturing large intraday moves more effectively and
more accurately than many timing systems used by day traders that
are based on traditional moving averages.

In order to visualize and apply this method to intraday price
moves, I use an eight-bar moving average of opening prices and an
eight-bar moving average of closing prices. Referring back to the
figures above, we can represent the open-versus-close relationship
using the eight-bar moving averages in a fashion that will allow us
to readily observe its efficacy and applications as timing triggers.

FIGURE 5.3

Google with an 8 open and an 8 close moving average. The arrow (top left) shows where the 8 close fell below 8 open, turning the trend bearish.

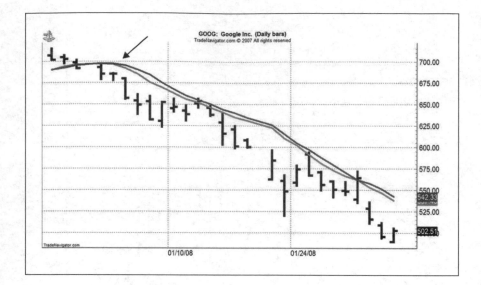

Surely things can't be as simple as illustrated in these figures. Remember that our work requires a setup, a trigger, and a follow through. Here is a brief summary of the methodology followed by clear and precise illustrations:

- Use 8 period MA of close.
- Use 8 period MA of open.
- In a bull market, most closes are higher than most opens.
- In a bear market, closes are usually lower than opens.
- The 8OC takes advantage of this important relationship.
- When 8 close goes above 8 open MA a buy is setup.
- For futures buy on a stop two ticks above the high of the setup bar.

- When 8 close goes below 8 open MA a sell is setup.
- For futures sell short on a stop two ticks below the low of the setup bar.
- For triggers in stocks I recommend 5 percent of the setup bar trading range.
- Remember that a setup is not a trigger. There may be many setups that reverse themselves the very next day without triggering.

Here are several exit strategies:

- The stop loss initially is the largest range price bar of the previous 10 bars, including the trigger bar.
- The profit target initially is the largest range bar of the previous 10 bars, including the trigger bar.
- The decision bar is bar number five if the position is profitable but has not reached its profit.
- The target at the end of bar number five is to liquidate a third of your position, trailing a stop of 75 percent on your second position, and placing a stop on the last position at breakeven, which is your original entry price.
- The decision bar is bar number five. If the trade is not profitable and has not been stopped out at the end of bar number five liquidate the entire position.
- After bar number five the trailing stop procedure described above goes into effect.
- Should a reversing trigger occur prior to bar number five, reverse your position.

Hold part of position for the big move; this is very important.

Now let's take a look at a few examples, complete with my setup, trigger, and follow through (STF) trading structure in various time frames before we examine the 8OC as a day trade, illustrating the fact that this method can be applied in any time frame and that the larger the time frame, the larger the potential profits.

FIGURE 5.4

Close/open in bull trend; arrow shows 8 close crossing
above 8 open prior to lengthy up move.

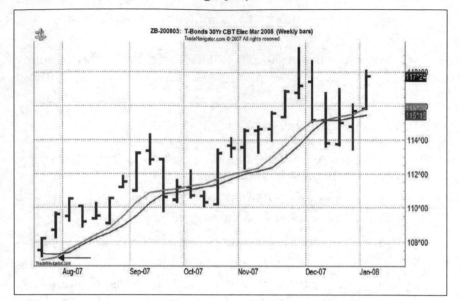

FIGURE 5.5

Google 8OC day trade

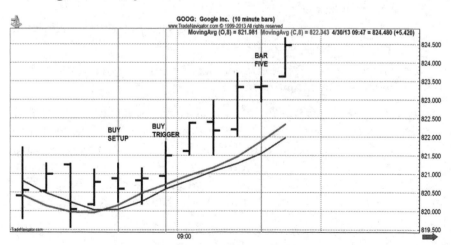

FIGURE 5.6

8 close/open in bear trend; in a market that is trending lower, the 8 MA of the close is often lower than the 8 MA of the opening.

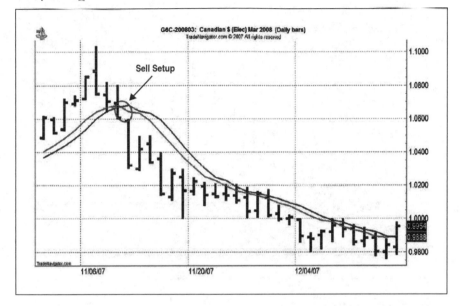

FIGURE 5.7

8 close/open; another example of the 8OC relationship

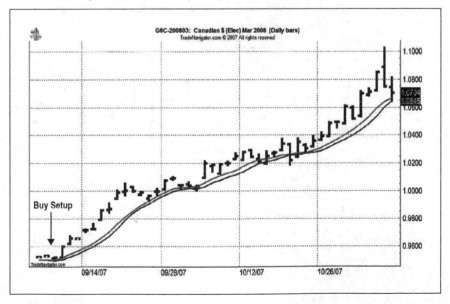

FIGURE 5.8

8 close/open, fifth bar pattern; at the fifth bar after a trigger (trigger bar counted as bar 1), a decision is made to either exit or take partial profit and hold the remainder of a trade.

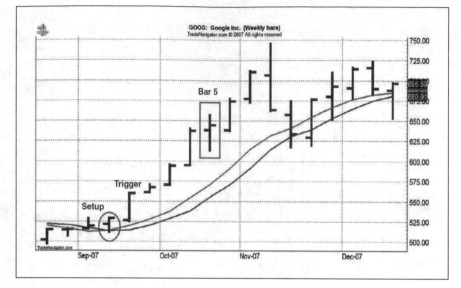

FIGURE 5.9

8 close/open, fifth bar pattern; at the fifth bar after a trigger (trigger bar counted as bar 1), a decision is made to either exit or take partial profit and hold the remainder of a trade.

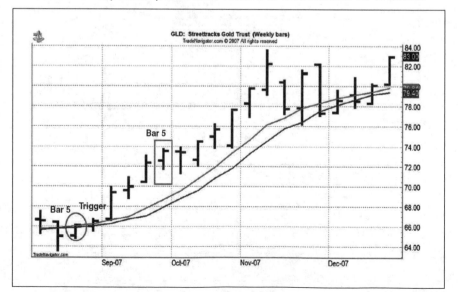

FIGURE 5.10

8OC with five bar pattern; at the fifth bar after a trigger (trigger bar counted as bar 1), a decision is made to either exit or take partial profit and hold the remainder of a trade.

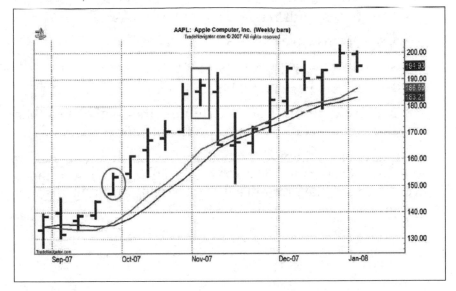

FIGURE 5.11

8OC with five bar pattern; at the fifth bar after a trigger (trigger bar counted as bar 1), a decision is made to either exit or take partial profit and hold the remainder of a trade.

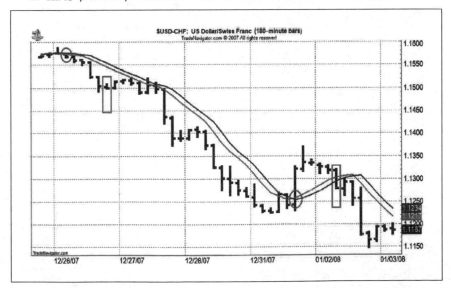

REVIEW OF 8OC RULES

- Buy trigger 8C > 8O
- Sell trigger 8C < 8O
- Exit strategy fifth bar partial profit or reversal
- Use only in active markets
- Use only in large price range markets
- Hold part of position for bigger moves
- Not useful for ultra-short-term time frames (i.e., less than five minutes) due to limited profit potential.

To summarize, the 8OC method is an excellent timing tool for short term and day trades. As in the case of all day trading methods I have developed, the profit-maximizing strategy is of the greatest importance.

CHAPTER 6

The MA Channel Method of Day Trading

The moving average channel (MAC) is a method I developed in the late 1970s. It was highly useful and effective then and is even better now. It is a very simple method to understand and just as simple to use.

THE METHOD

The MAC is based on two simple moving averages (MAs). As opposed to the use of traditional moving average crossover systems, which use the moving average of closing prices, the MAC uses two MAs, one MA of the high price and one MA of the low price. In testing the historical performance of traditional closing MA systems, the typical results with such crossovers systems are very poor, usually in the range of 30 to 45 percent accuracy. The MAC improves the odds considerably because it is a total method, using my setup, trigger, and follow through (STF) approach and it does not use closing prices.

Here are the basic rules of application for the MAC. Additional aspects will be discussed later on.

- Calculate an 8-period simple MA of the low price for each bar (i.e., daily, weekly, or intraday).

- Calculate a 10-period simple MA of the high price for each bar (i.e., daily, weekly, or intraday).

- A *buy* setup occurs when *two* complete bars are *above* the MA of the high (MAH).

- A *buy* trigger occurs when the trigger indictor (Williams AD/MA) crosses. To be discussed below.

- A *sell* setup occurs when *two* complete consecutive bars are *below* the MA of the low (MAL).

- All setups must be triggered (see below).

- *The price bars must be completely above or below the MA line to be valid. Note this carefully: the entire bar must be outside the channel.*

All of the above can be easily done by computer charting software. I use Williams Accumulation and a simple 57-period MA of Williams. Williams crossing above its MA confirms a buy, and Williams crossing below its MA confirms a sell. The two bars above or below setup must coincide with the related crossovers noted above. The examples provided below will clarify the rules.

Use 2 simple MAs:

- MAH=10 periods of the high

- MAL= 8 periods of the low

- *Two* complete consecutive price bars above MAH is a buy pattern (use confirmation for a trigger)

- *Two* complete consecutive price bars below MAL is a sell pattern (use confirmation for a trigger)

- Confirmation is required using the Williams AD/MA

- Use Williams AD with simple 57-period MA of Williams AD

MOVING AVERAGE CHANNEL BREAKOUT

As opposed to the use of traditional moving average crossover methods, which use the MA of closing prices, the MAC uses two MAs, one of the high price and one of the low. As previously noted, typical results with MA-based methods that use closing prices are very poor, usually in the range of 30 to 45 percent accuracy. MAC improves the odds considerably because it is a total method that uses the STF approach. Rather than using MAs of closing prices, the MAC uses MAs of highs and lows combined with a price bar pattern and a confirming indicator or trigger (Williams AD and its MA). A moving average channel breakout (MACB) occurs when there are two successive price bars above the MAC high or below the MAC low. Here are a few examples of MACB signals (see Figure 6.1 to 6.3).

- First Profit Target=2 × MA channel on trigger day.

- Stop loss=2 × MA channel on trigger day.

- When target is hit, exit one-third of position. Lock in 75 percent of profit with trailing stop and stop last third at breakeven (entry price).

- Hold with breakeven stop until a reversing MAC sell signal occurs.

MAC SWING TRADE

The moving average channel continuation (MACC or swing trade) method uses the MAC to buy at defined support in uptrends and sell at MAC resistance in downtrends.

MACC indicators are as follows:

- 8-period simple moving average of the low.

- 10-period simple moving average of the high.

- Williams AD.

- 57-period simple moving average of Williams AD.

MACC rules are as follows:

- Buy setup two consecutive bars above the 10-period MA of the high and Williams AD > its 57 MA.

- Buy trigger price moves down to the 8-period MA of the low.

FIGURE 6.1

MAC signals on a daily price chart

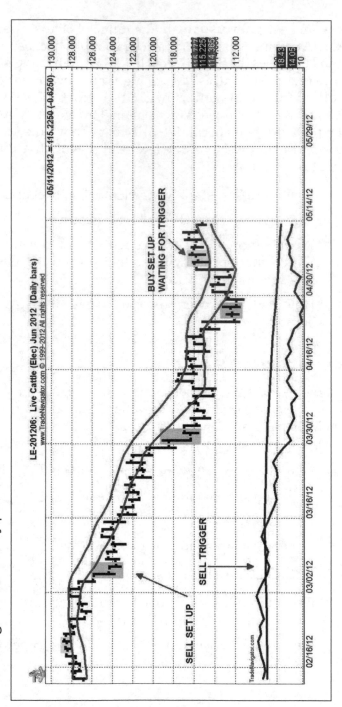

LE-201206: Live Cattle (Elec) Jun 2012 (Daily bars)
www.TradeNavigator.com © 1999-2012 All rights reserved

FIGURE 6.2

MAC signals on an intraday price chart of E-Mini S&P futures

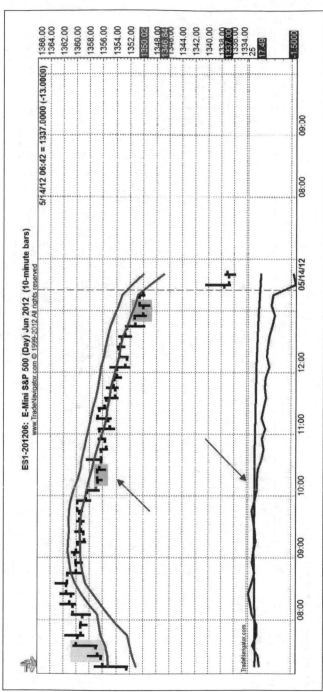

FIGURE 6.3

MAC signals on an intraday price chart of European currency futures

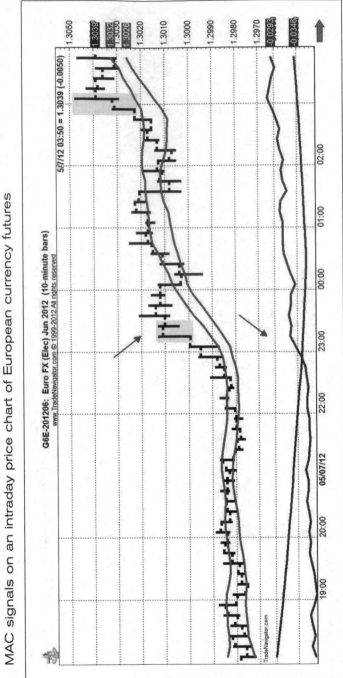

G6E-201206: Euro FX (Elec) Jun 2012 (10-minute bars)
www.TradeNavigator.com © 1999-2012 All rights reserved

5/7/12 03:50 = 1.3039 (-0.0050)

- Sell trigger is two consecutive bars below the 8-period MA of the low and Williams AD < its 57 MA.

- Sell swing trade price moves up to the 10-period MA of the high.

- First profit target = the width of the channel as measured on the day the trade is entered.

- Stop loss = twice the width of the channel as measured on the day the trade is entered *or* a reversing MACB setup and trigger.

Here are some examples of the MACC on several charts.

More MACC Details

The examples above make the MAC method seem easy. There's a lot more to the MAC than I have shown you to this point. Here are a few more very important aspects, all of which are illustrated in detail below.

- When the MAC has triggered a buy, the MAL serves as support in the new uptrend. In other words, in an uptrend you can buy at support.

- When the MAC has triggered a sell, the MAH serves as resistance in the new downtrend. In other words, in a downtrend you can sell at resistance.

- The more consecutive bars that comprise a new signal, the more significant the new trend is likely to be.

- A narrowing channel in an uptrend tends to precede a correction down or a possible top.

- A widening channel in an uptrend tends to precede a sharp rally.

- A narrowing channel in a downtrend tends to precede a correction up or a possible bottom.

- A widening channel in a downtrend tends to precede a sharp decline.

FIGURE 6.4

MAC swing trade

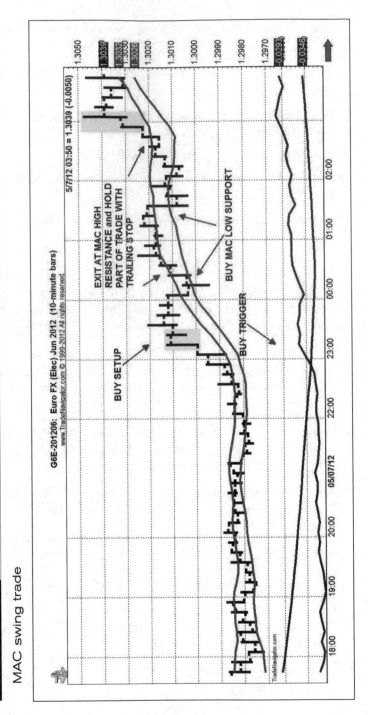

G6E-201206: Euro FX (Elec) Jun 2012 (10-minute bars)
www.TradeNavigator.com © 1999-2012 All rights reserved

5/7/12 03:50 = 1.3039 (-0.0050)

BUY SETUP

EXIT AT MAC HIGH
RESISTANCE and HOLD
PART OF TRADE WITH
TRAILING STOP

BUY MAC LOW SUPPORT

BUY TRIGGER

FIGURE 6.5

MAC swing trade sell points in downtrend

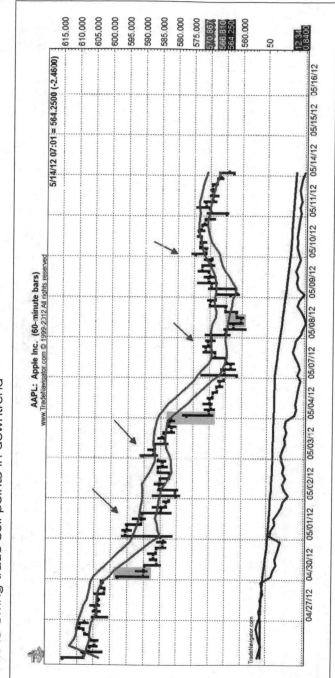

FIGURE 6.6

MAC swing trade buy points in T-Bond futures

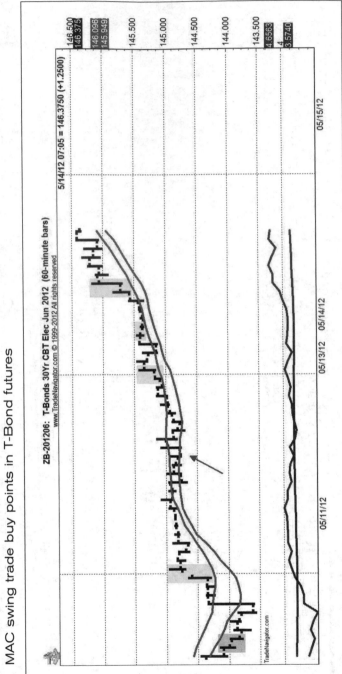

Here are two examples of the conditions noted above:

In summary, the MAC is a highly versatile method that has a variety of applications that are not mutually exclusive; you can apply all of them at the same time. The way in which you do so is up to you.

Here are some important tips for using the MAC successfully:

- Use the MAC in active markets only. If a market is thinly traded, the price bars will be small and the accuracy of the MAC will be poor. If you use the daily price chart for futures, use the lead month or active month.

- If you use the MAC in the intraday time frame, I recommend you not use it for time frames of less than 10 minutes.

- Remember that when you use the MAC swing trading method, your profits will be limited as a function of the width of the channel for the given market(s) you are trading.

- The MAC methods require experience and should not be used in a totally mechanical fashion. Get some experience before you attempt to use them.

- The MAC can be used as a breakout method or as a swing trade method. Examples of both applications have been given earlier in this chapter. The swing trade method which is often more appealing to day traders is detailed in Chapter 7. Both methods are compatible, meaning they are not muturally exclusive. You can do both at the same time. The swing trade will give you more trades but the breakout trade may give you larger profits with less work.

FIGURE 6.7

MACC swing trade

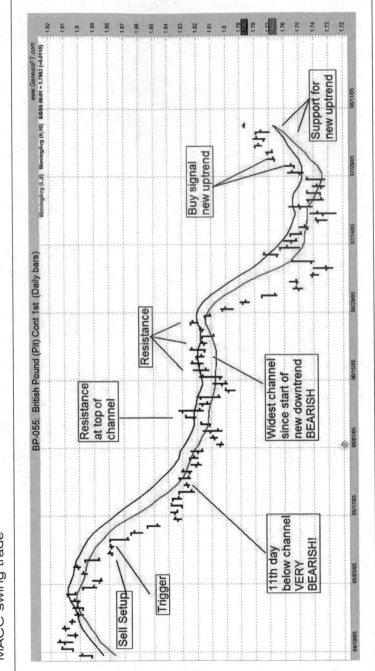

FIGURE 6.8

MACC swing trade

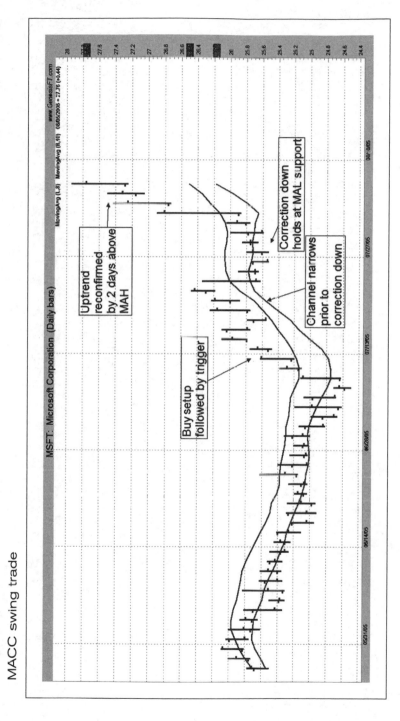

CHAPTER 7

Day Trade Swing Trade Examples in Stocks, Futures, and Forex

Many newcomers to day trading, as well as experienced traders who wish to learn more about swing trading, are often disappointed in the lack of detailed information and methodologies they find. Although an Internet search of the term *swing trading* yields over 15 million possibilities. The available information on all aspects of day trading, while plentiful, is neither clear nor effective. Rarely will you find precise procedures and operational definitions that will be of true value in your day trading endeavors. Accordingly, I have dedicated this chapter to a close examination of swing day trade signals in various markets and time frames. Note that a "swing trade" by my definition is a trade that is implemented at a support or resistance level. It is therefore necessary to define support and resistance operationally.

Let's begin with Figure 7.1, which shows the 30-minute intra-day price bars for the SPY using the MAC method with Williams AD and it's moving average (MA) of 57. The chart indicates the following:

- The vertical line at the left shows the complete consecutive price bars below the bottom of the MAC, accompanied by Williams AD below its MA. This is a new sell trigger. Resistance is defined as the MAC high.

- Shortly thereafter (rectangle) prices reach the top of the channel (resistance), where a short sale would be implemented, thereafter reaching the bottom of the channel, where a short position would be exited.

- Thereafter the top of the MAC is hit a number of times with prices coming back down to the bottom of the channel, each of these constituting a profitable swing trade from the short side.

- For three consecutive days there were opportunities to sell at resistance, the MAC high, and to close out the position support, the MAC low.

Throughout this book I have stressed the importance of capturing the larger moves by maintaining part of a position after exit using a trailing stop loss. As you can see from my downward-sloping arrow after the last sell opportunity, there were no new resistance points at which to sell short; however, a large move down continued as the bearish trend became entrenched. This is the type of move that I'm referring to when I talk about the bigger move. In this case the only way to capture this large move would have been to hold the position beyond the course of the day, which would classify this trade as a short-term one as opposed to a day trade.

It should come as no surprise that the stock of Apple computer (AAPL) would move in the direction of the broader market during the same time as the decline in SPY, as demonstrated in Figure 7.1. An examination of Figure 7.2 shows the following:

- The vertical line at the left on May 14, 2012, shows the start of a downtrend, according to the MAC rules.

- On May 15 the top of the MAC was touched a number of times, and in each case the bottom of the MAC was then hit, making for profitable swing day trades.

- No opportunities to sell short using this method occurred on May 16 or 17.

- On May 18 the MAC was hit and exceeded, followed almost immediately by a strong decline to about $522 per share.

- This profitable opportunity was followed by yet another opportunity to sell at the top of the MAC and to close out the trade at the MAC low for yet another profitable swing trade on May 18.

FIGURE 7.1

MAC swing trade signals in 30-minute SPY

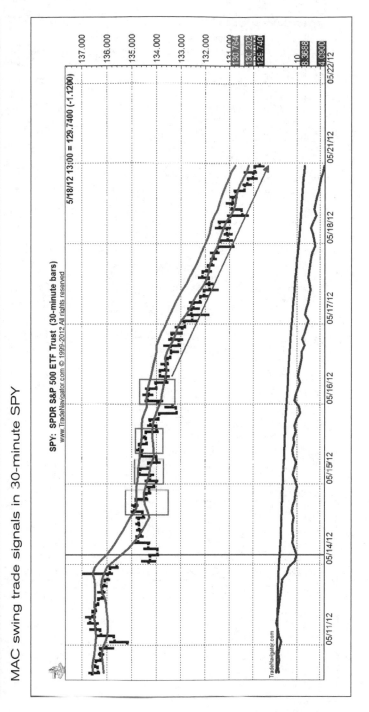

SPY: SPDR S&P 500 ETF Trust (30-minute bars)
www.TradeNavigator.com © 1999-2012 All rights reserved

5/18/12 13:00 = 129.7400 (-1.1200)

FIGURE 7.2

MAC swing trade signals in 30-minute AAPL

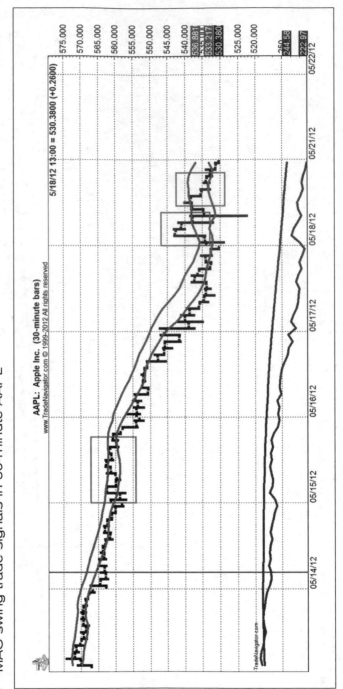

AAPL: Apple Inc. (30-minute bars)
www.TradeNavigator.com © 1999-2012 All rights reserved

Figure 7.3 shows my MAC swing day trades in the ES1 180-minute chart. Here are the salient points from the chart:

- On May 11 the top of MAC was hit for a sell short swing trade because it turned negative on May 4.

- This trade was closed out the same day, May 11, at the bottom of the MAC for profit.

- As in previous cases, the trend continued down for a substantial move after a short position was closed out. However, as indicated earlier, to capture such large profits would have necessitated holding the trade beyond the day session, so it would no longer be a day trade but rather a short-term one.

Figure 7.4 shows the 360-minute wheat chart with my MAC setup and trigger. The vertical line on May 17 shows the trigger. Clearly because there was no pullback to MAC support, there were no swing day trade opportunities. On the other hand, simply buying this market on the signal without waiting for a pullback to support would have yielded good profits over the next several days. Not all buy or sell triggers will give us swing trade a opportunity.

As mentioned previously, there is a growing issue regarding what constitutes a day for day trade purposes. With Forex, which trades 24 hours a day, the definition of the day is different for day trade purposes than it would be in other markets. If you want to stay awake 24 hours and trade all day, you have your work cut out for you. On a more rational level, I suggest you use a six-hour chart (so you can get some sleep between trades) such as the one shown in Figure 7.5, in which I have marked with a rectangle the drops to MAC support in an uptrend to help you examine how the signals worked. Note that in all cases shown above, prices eventually went back up to MAC resistance, where profits would be taken according to the rules of the MAC swing trade method.

Figure 7.6 shows MAC swing trade possibilities in the U.S. dollar vs. Canadian dollar Forex trade. The rectangle shows numerous declines to MAC support with rallies thereafter to MAC resistance during the course of an uptrending market that was triggered on May 7, where I show the vertical line. As in previous cases, the move continued higher for several days thereafter, which again

FIGURE 7.3

MAC swing trade signals in 180-minute ES1 (S&P E-Mini day session futures)

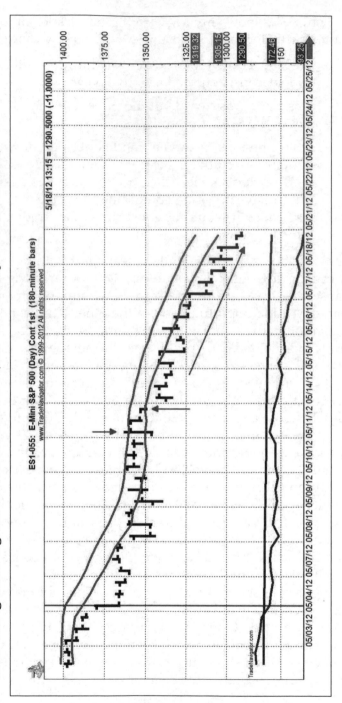

FIGURE 7.4

MAC swing trade signals in 360-minute wheat

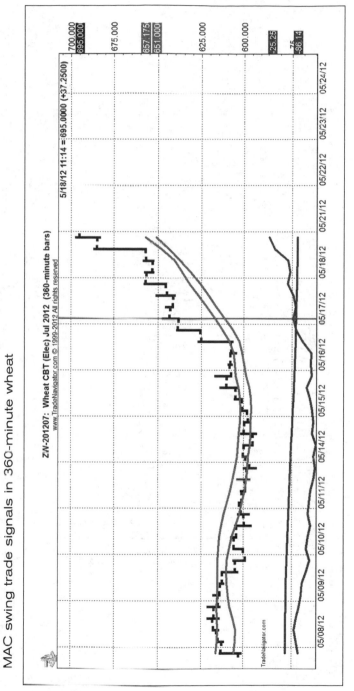

ZN-201207: Wheat CBT (Elec) Jul 2012 (360-minute bars)
www.TradeNavigator.com © 1999-2012 All rights reserved

5/18/12 11:14 =695.0000 (+37.2500)

FIGURE 7.5

MAC swing trade signals in 360-minute Euro/USD Forex trade

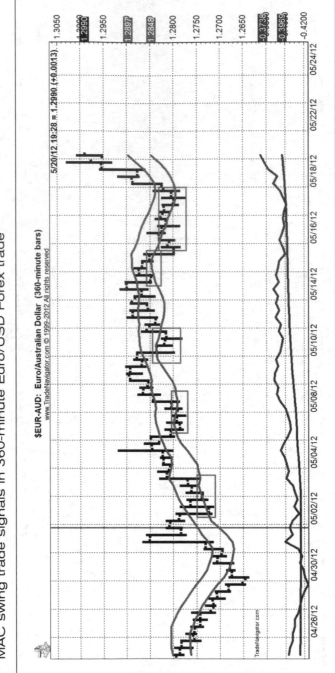

$EUR-AUD: Euro/Australian Dollar (360-minute bars)
www.TradeNavigator.com © 1999-2012 All rights reserved

5/20/12 19:28 = 1.2990 (+0.0013)

Tradebigator.com

FIGURE 7.6

MAC swing trade signals in 360-minute USD/CAD Forex trade

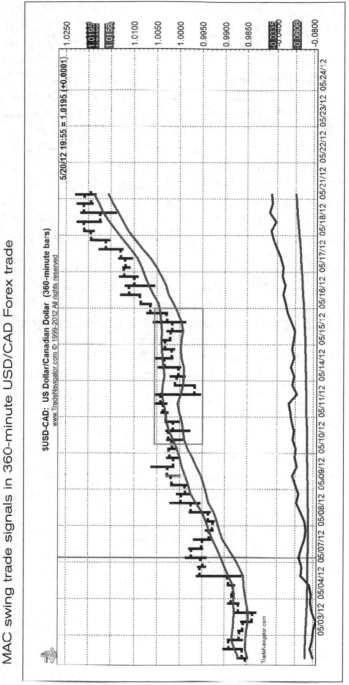

$USD-CAD: US Dollar/Canadian Dollar (360-minute bars)
www.TradeNavigator.com © 1999-2012 All rights reserved

5/20/12 19:55 = 1.0195 (+0.0001)

underscores my oft-repeated suggestion that in order to make big money you must be in for the bigger move, and that the bigger move is one that you can only get by using a trailing stop on the last part of your position and holding beyond the end of the session.

Another consideration in day trading is the length of time in which you want to trade. You can make many choices, all the way from tick-by-tick charts to one-minute charts to six-hour charts. Many traders are under the incorrect impression that shorter-term time frames will yield more opportunities. While that may very well be true, profitable day trading is not a function of opportunities as much as it is of sufficiently large opportunities in order to allow for a reasonable profit. As an example, consider Figure 7.7, which shows a five-minute chart in a Forex pair. I have marked the channel width to indicate the profit potential and channel high to channel low. As you can see, the range is very small, which would mean that in order to profit after commission charges your position size needs to be large. Always consider the size of the channel in determining the time frame for your chart.

Figure 7.8 offers a classic example of how swing trades to sell at the top of the channel can continue for an extended period of time. With the exception of the last trade shown on the right-hand side of the chart, where the MAC and the two-bar pattern turned bullish, all indicated trades would have been profitable selling at the MAC high and exiting positions at the MAC low or lower.

FIGURE 7.7

MAC swing trade signals in 360-minute Euro/USD Forex trade

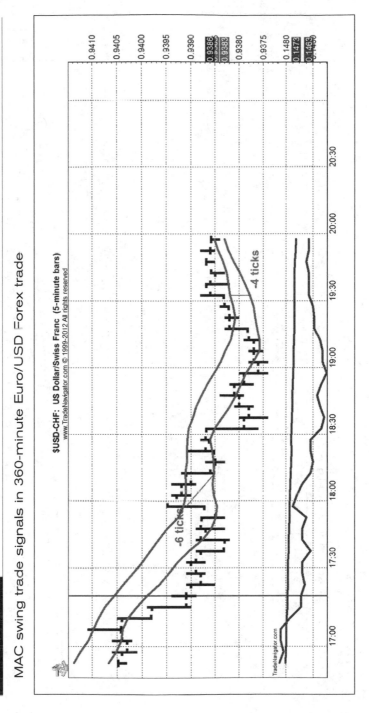

FIGURE 7.8

MAC swing trade signals in 180-minute Euro/USD futures trade

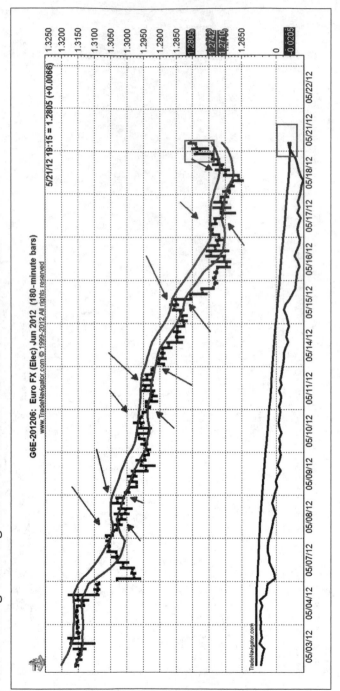

G6E-201206: Euro FX (Elec) Jun 2012 (180-minute bars)
www.TradeNavigator.com © 1999-2012 All rights reserved

5/21/12 19:15 = 1.2805 (+0.0066)

CHAPTER 8

The 30-Minute Breakout

Several years after the start of trading in S&P futures, I introduced my 30-minute breakout (30 MBO) trading method. The method was designed to capture the large intraday price swings in S&P futures in an objective and organized fashion, in sharp contrast to the seat-of-the-pants methods used by most traders at that time. Unfortunately many S&P day traders today also make decisions on emotion and interpretation rather than procedures and rules.

My development of the 30 MBO method was based on a simple observation. After many days of watching S&P futures, I observed that the first half-hour trading range was often a period of support and resistance development that if penetrated subsequent to the end of that period tended to produce moves in the direction of the penetration or breakout. My point was to develop a methodology designed to consistently capture those moves.

Over the years there have been many attempts by other traders and educators to refine my method, most of them unsuccessful and, sadly, many of them claiming to be the originators of the method. In spite of the fact that the 30 MBO has been around for so many years, just a few days ago, one of my students made me aware of the latest attempt to claim credit for this trading approach. Many of the imitators get the approach completely wrong, so *caveat emptor*!

OVERVIEW

The 30 MBO method uses the first 30-minute range of the day session E-Mini S&P futures. It is important to use only the day session E-Mini S&P futures data because this is a market that trades effectively all day and night. As indicated previously, the definition of the day trade for our purposes is the day session in futures and/or stocks.

Once a 30-minute high and low range of the E-Mini S&P futures has been established, a buy trigger occurs if on any 30-minute price bar thereafter the ending price is higher than the high price of the first 30-minute bar. A sell trigger occurs if on any 30-minute bar subsequent to the first 30-minute bar closing price or ending price is below the low of the first 30-minute price bar. A long or a short position is entered at the market. The first profit target (PT 1) is 50 percent of the price range of the first 30-minute bar. The full profit target (PT 2) is a full range of the first 30-minute bar. The stop loss for a long trade is a reversing short trade, and the stop loss for a short trade is a reversing long trade. If you find this difficult to follow, rest assured my illustrations will make everything clear.

Units

I prefer to trade the 30-minute breakout in units of three: 3, 6, 9, 12 futures contracts or, if you trade in the SPY, 300 shares, 600 shares, 900 shares, etc. Profit targets one and two are exited according to the rules, whereas profit target three must be closed up by the end of the day as a flexible exit strategy. This is where the art and science, or if you prefer experience, comes into play.

Considerations

On occasion the first 30-minute bar is very large. This tends to occur if there is important news when the market opens. I find that if the trading range of the first 30-minute bar is 10 full S&P points or more than the probability, then the probability of a successful outcome for breakout trade is fairly low. Remember, when dealing with any of my methods you must consider your risk beyond anything.

It should also be noted that the stop loss for the initial position is a reversing signal, which means that there must be a close below the first 30-minute low if you are long or a close above the first 30-minute high if you're short. At times this can result in a loss that is much bigger than was expected.

Profit-Maximizing Strategy

As in all day trading methods, the most important ingredient for success is the profit-maximizing strategy. Unless you can consistently maintain a very high accuracy level with an average profit considerably larger than your average loss, your profits on the bottom line will be a function of what you make on the big trade. You can believe me now, or you can believe me later. The big trade is usually the last trade. Having said that, the last trade may also cause you the most frustration. The reasons for this will become abundantly clear as I go through some chart examples to illustrate the 30 MBO as well as the profit-maximizing strategy.

A FEW THINGS TO CONSIDER

As is the case for all methods described in this book, there are some important things to consider before you begin trading with the 30 MBO.

The Most Volatile Game in Town

Day trading is the most volatile game in town. I'm sure you already know that, but just to reinforce and reiterate the idea as a "public health warning" be advised that in today's extremely volatile markets, the large up-and-down moves within the course of the day in stocks, as well as in futures, create opportunity as well as risk. Do not be drawn to day trading in S&P futures, or in stocks for that matter, simply by the opportunity. Consider the risk as well. In addition, consider the other factors stated below and determine whether playing the most volatile game in town is right for you. Remember also that risk can be mitigated by trading smaller-sized futures contracts, by trading options, or by trading individual stocks such as the SPY for the 30 MBO.

You Will Need to Be There Every Day

I get many e-mails and telephone calls from traders who want to earn a living at day trading, but for various and sundry reasons cannot *be there* to play the game every day. My advice is as follows:

1. You *can* play the game without being at the computer daily, depending on the method you use. For example, the gap trade could be implemented on any day as long as you are able to follow through with the method correctly and completely.

2. If you trade the 30 MBO, it is best to do so every day; if you can't do that, try to do it on the same day(s) every week, in case there is a day-of-the-week pattern.

3. Do not try to day trade while you are on vacation or away from the computer for extended periods of time when you should be there to mind your day trade(s).

Return on Effort: Is the Game Worth Playing?

Every business or venture has its learning curve. Day trading is no different. At first your return on effort either will be minimal or you will lose money. The most likely possibility is that you will lose money while you learn the game. If and when you begin making money day trading, you must ask yourself whether the game is worth playing. Consider the time and effort you put into playing the game; are you getting a return that justifies your effort, or would you be making as much money working at a fast-food restaurant? If you find that your methods are producing money consistently and your bottom line is improving after several months but not dramatically so in terms of profits, a simple way to proceed is to trade larger positions. If you trade larger positions, however, you must be able to finance those positions with sufficient margin, and you must also be willing to take the larger degree of risk. For some traders increasing position size puts the kibosh on their success. Be aware of position size and know your limits.

Large Intraday Price Swings Can Work
For or Against You

All too often traders are attracted to the markets by the promise of profits and the lure of large intraday price moves. They
prefer to trade markets that have large price swings during the
day because they're blinded by the light of profits. I remind you
that large intraday price swings can work for or against you. Not
only do they improve the potential profit, they also increase sub-
stantially the potential loss. Remember that in evaluating profits,
risk, and volatility, your credo should be "the bigger the front,
the bigger the back."

Know Your Competition

If you were asked to play poker in Las Vegas at a high-stakes
game, one of the first things you'd want to know is who
your competition would be. Indeed, a beginner should know
that if you are competing against professional gamblers, your
odds of winning would be slim to none. When it comes to
day trading, however, most individuals do not consider this
question. Rest assured, if you are trying to win at the day
trading game, you are competing against some of the best and
most experienced traders in the world. Not only are you competing with individuals who have much more experience than you,
you are also competing against individuals who have better tools
than you do. High-frequency traders have access to information,
technology, and software that far exceed almost anything the
newcomer has in his arsenal of trading tools. These individuals
can frequently make considerable money every day on extremely
small moves no matter what the market may be as long as
it has liquidity. If you know that you have stiff competition
and that your odds of winning against such competition are
very low, you will be more attentive to what you do, more
vigilant about risk management, more aggressive about profit-
maximizing strategies, and more conscientious about learning
the game before you place. What I have just told you is perhaps
one of the most important things you need to know before you
begin day trading.

If You're a Beginner, Why Start with the Hardest Game in Town?

In addition to being aware of your competition, you must also consider that day trading is the most difficult of all market games. It is not only difficult because it requires effective techniques, vigilant execution of trades, adherence to methodology, and strict management of losses and risk, but given the competition, it is also the most difficult game in town because exit at the end of the day is required. That means you'll need to take your remaining profit or loss at the end of the day and there are no excuses. You can easily go wrong by assuming your loss will turn around if you do not exit, or that your profit will get larger if you stay in the game overnight. That is the worst thing you could do. Rather than beginning your trading venture with the most difficult game in town trading the S&P, the most difficult market in town, you might want to start with a market that is more tame or has less risk. You might want to consider Treasury bond or Treasury note futures. You might want to consider the Forex market, in which you can determine the size of the position you want to take. You might want to consider micro or other currency futures. You might want to consider gold or silver futures. Some of these may be more suited to your financial condition, risk tolerance, and level of experience. Why? Because in many cases they will not move as quickly as S&P futures, and when they do move against you, the dollar risk will not be as high.

Know Your Personal Tolerance Level

You must be aware of your tolerance level. How much of a move against you can you realistically handle emotionally as well as financially? How quickly do you cave in and lose your discipline? How stable are you emotionally when it comes to winning and losing? Do you get easily carried away by profits and hold on to positions beyond the exit points? How well do you know yourself when it comes to trading? These are all considerations that must be taken into account before you trade. Note, however, that you will not know the answers to these questions until you actually step into the water and get your toes wet. One of the most important things I can tell traders may sound incredibly simple, but I believe it is incredibly powerful: "Don't trade anything that scares you."

SYNOPSIS OF RULES

Before going on to specific historical examples of 30 MBO trades, here is a summary of the rules, with some commentary about each of them.

Day Session Only

The 30 MBO is traded in the ES1 futures or SPY stock. If you study the method and find it effective in other markets, you can apply it there as well. But only day session hours are used for generating trades. I repeat: only day session hours are used for this method.

First 30-Minute Bar: Do Not Trade

The first 30 minutes of trading of the day session is used to set up buy and sell trigger points. If you want to use this method successfully, do not trade during the first 30 minutes. It is only at the end of the first 30-minute bar that a decision can be made about buy and sell trigger points. Even then, after the 30-minute session is over, we cannot make a buy or sell trigger decision until the end of the second half-hour bar at the very earliest. Penetration of the buy or sell points after the first 30-minute bar but during the next or any subsequent bar does not constitute a buy or sell trigger. The buy or sell trigger can only occur at the end of the bar, not during the bar. This is critically important to my method. Beware: some of the individuals who have literally stolen my 30 MBO method advise buying or selling on any penetration of the 30-minute bar high or low. I believe that doing so will get you into trouble, causing you many false trades as well as losses.

At the End of the First 30 Minutes

Now is the time to make note of the 30-minute high and low. These levels become your buy and sell triggers. I reiterate: in order to implement my 30 MBO successfully, do nothing for the first 30 minutes of the day session, then note the 30-minute bar high and low exactly, and use them as your buy and sell trigger points.

Buy on 30-minute "Close" above Buy Trigger

A close above the 30-minute high triggers a buy at the market, and a close below the first 30-minute low triggers a sell at the market. If and when you get a buy trigger, implement a strategy at the market. Do not attempt to wait for a better price execution. To do so means you will often miss a trading opportunity.

Sell Short on 30-Minute "Close" below Sell Trigger

When I say sell short on 30-minute close below the sell trigger, I mean to do so specifically at the market. Some traders will attempt to wait in order to try to get a better price execution. I have found this to be ineffective; it will often cause you to miss trading opportunities.

First Profit Target Is 50 Percent of Range of First 30-Minute Bar

Your first profit target will be 50 percent of the range of the first 30 minutes. As an example, if the range from high to low of the first 30-minute bar is 840 points, your first target will be 420 points. If you are a more aggressive trader, you will wait for the full profit target to be achieved rather than the first profit target. My original method was to wait for the entire range of the first 30-minute bar as a profit target. Significantly increased volatility in S&P has necessitated the 50 percent range target. Some of the illustrations in this chapter show the full range of profit target one and subsequent profit targets to be the same range as profit target one, while others show 50 percent as the target. My suggestion is to wait and watch the markets to see what works best for you. If you use 50 percent as the first profit target, liquidate one-third of your position with an open order at that price, and if you have two-thirds of your position remaining, trail a stop loss on one position at 75 percent of the maximum move from entry; another stop should remain a breakeven in the event that the market keeps moving in your favor. In the event that a very large move in your favor occurs subsequent to your first profit target being hit, you can implement a more aggressive stop. In any event, you must be out of your last position market on close.

Full Target Is Entire Range of First 30-Minute Bar

After you have read my comments regarding the 50 percent profit target and the full profit target, do your own studies to see which method is best for you. If you use the full range of the first 30-minute bar as your target, exit one-third of your position at that point and use a 75 percent trailing stop and a breakeven stop strategy as discussed earlier for the remainder of your positions.

Stop Loss Is the Opposite Side of the Trade

The initial stop loss on the 30 MBO is the opposite side of the trade. By this I mean that if you have a buy trigger first, you're stopped and risk becomes the sell trigger. If you have a sell trigger first, your stop and risk becomes the buy trigger. If you have a sell followed by a buy later in the day, you would reverse your position and expose yourself to two possible losses. This is a real and ever-present danger in this method, and you must prepare for the possibility. Remember also that the stop loss initially would be a closing below the 30-minute low if you are long or closing above the 30-minute high if you are short. This is very important because during the 30-minute bar the opposite trade or trigger level may be penetrated, but by the end of the bar that will have been no signal. This means that you are exposed to a loss that might be much larger than expected during the 30 minutes you're waiting for a possible reversal and stop signal. Depending upon the instrument you are trading, you could mitigate this potential loss by buying an option position to protect you.

THE MOST CRITICAL ASPECT IS THE FOLLOW THROUGH

I cannot overstate the fact that follow through by the rules is critically important for success using the 30 MBO. As a reminder, follow through means 100 percent or as close to 100 percent as possible implementation of buy and sell triggers, initial stop loss, trailing stop losses, and end of day exit. It's that simple and that complicated. That could be said for all methods, of course, but it is especially important in the 30 MBO. Two elements, profit-maximizing strategy and exiting part of your position of the first profit target to reduce risk, are the most important. Just as the right follow through is important to the professional athlete, it is also what brings success to the professional trader. Here is an item-by-item review of 30 MBO follow through, as well as some suggestions for maximizing profit and minimizing risk.

- Trade in units of three (i.e., three, six, nine, twelve, etc.). In futures that means trading in units of three contracts, and in stock units of 300 shares. This allows you to exit partial positions at PT1 and/or PT2 to reduce risk and maximize profits.

- Exit one unit at PT1 and reduce your risk effectively to zero!

- PT1=range of first 30-minute bar for the aggressive trader, 50 percent of this range for the conservative trader.

- When PT1 is hit and profit is taken on one-third of position, raise stop loss on one of the two remaining units to your entry price at one to 75 percent trailing stop. Remember that by trailing stop, I mean 75 percent of the profits being locked in as measured from the entry price to the extreme high of the move if long or the extreme low of the move if short.

- When PT2 is hit, raise stop on one unit to PT1 and keep stop loss on one unit at breakeven.

- There are many variations on the theme of profit-maximizing strategy. After you have experience with the 30 MBO, you will develop your own profit-maximizing strategies that may be better for you.

- The more units you trade, the more flexibility you will have in your exit strategy. The more flexible you are in your exit strategy, the more likely you will be able to ride large profits once such moves occur.

Additional Aspects

- Hold one unit for exit MOC (market on close) if not stopped out. Frequently this will be your largest winning position.

- *Do not carry* after the end of the day session. A day trade is a day trade. You entered your trade with the intention of exiting by the end of the session, win, lose, or draw, so the trade must be closed out that day. Too many traders have seen their profits disappear literally overnight.

- I've often been asked whether there is a way to maximize profits by carrying positions beyond the end of the day into the 24-hour session. The first thing I would tell you is that in so doing you may not qualify for day trade margins, as you had with your broker. I would also say is a okay to do it on part of your position, assuming this winning position and assuming you placed a trailing stop on the position in the event that the trade reverses in the after-day-hours market.

- Although the 30 MBO was developed exclusively for use in S&P futures, some traders have told me it works in the electronic day session NASDAQ or the QQQ. I have no research or opinion regarding their claims.

- 30 MBO can also be used in Russell Mini (ER1). See my comments about the NASDAQ above.

- 30 MBO can also be used in the Dow, but base Dow trades on S&P triggers.

- 30 MBO can also be traded with OEX options as a defined risk alternative.

- 30 MBO is *not* related to the underlying trend of the market.

- If a setup does not trigger by the last 90 minutes of trading, it is too late to enter and there is no trade for that day.

ILLUSTRATIONS AND COMMENTARY

Figure 8.1 shows the ideal configuration of the 30 MBO setup and trigger on the buy side, with a trigger on price bar number three with follow through.

Figure 8.2 is the ideal configuration of the 30 MBO setup and trigger on the sell side, showing a trigger on price bar number five with follow through.

Figure 8.3 is the ideal configuration of the 30 MBO setup and trigger on the sell side, taken from an actual trading day as opposed to the ideal schematic shown in Figures 8.1and 8.2. It shows a trigger on price bar number two with follow through at the full range of bar number one as the profit target and subsequent profit targets as the same amount as the first bar range. Using the 50 percent of bar number one target, the results would have been profitable as well.

Figure 8.4 shows three consecutive 30 MBO trades, each of which triggered early in the day and achieved profit targets. On the first day shown (August 25, 2008), a trigger occurred in bar number three and the trade quickly went on to achieve all profit targets. On the next day the trigger occurred on bar number two and the trade

FIGURE 8.1

30 MBO buy setup and trigger

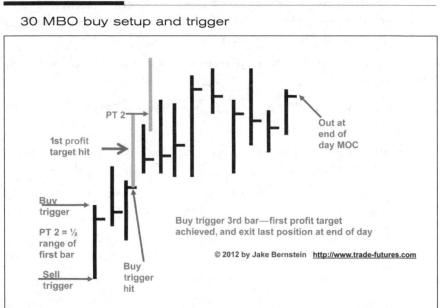

PT 2

1st profit target hit

Buy trigger

PT 2 = ½ range of first bar

Sell trigger

Buy trigger hit

Out at end of day MOC

Buy trigger 3rd bar—first profit target achieved, and exit last position at end of day

© 2012 by Jake Bernstein   http://www.trade-futures.com

FIGURE 8.2

30 MBO sell setup and trigger

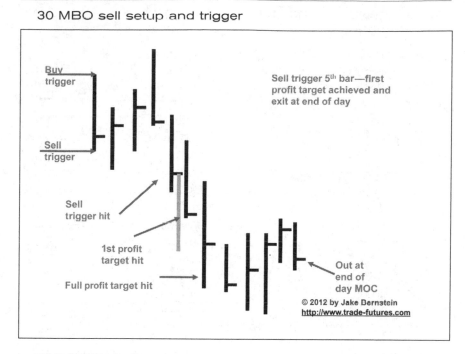

Buy trigger

Sell trigger

Sell trigger 5th bar—first profit target achieved and exit at end of day

Sell trigger hit

1st profit target hit

Full profit target hit

Out at end of day MOC

© 2012 by Jake Bernstein
http://www.trade-futures.com

FIGURE 8.3

Actual sell trade

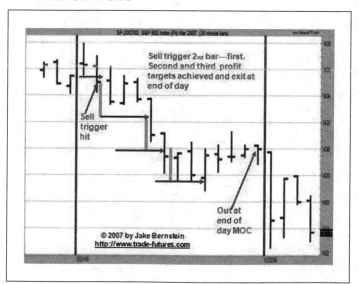

Sell trigger 2nd bar—first. Second and third profit targets achieved and exit at end of day

Sell trigger hit

Out at end of day MOC

© 2007 by Jake Bernstein
http://www.trade-futures.com

FIGURE 8.4

Three consecutive 30 MBO trades, 8/25/08

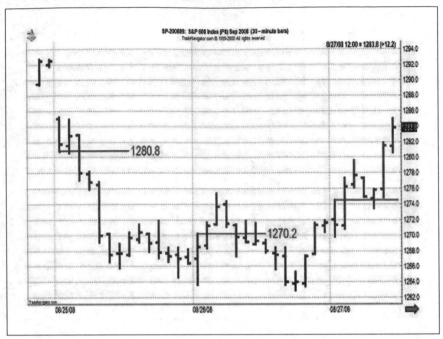

quickly went on to barely achieve its first profit target, which was 50 percent of the range of the first bar. On day number three, a trigger occurred on the second bar and prices then quickly went on to achieve all profit targets before the end of the day.

Figure 8.5 shows three consecutive 30 MBO trades, each of which triggered early in the day and achieved profit targets. On the first day shown (August 27, 2008), a trigger occurred in bar number two and the trade went on to eventually achieve all profit targets. On the next day, the trigger occurred on bar number three and the trade went on to barely achieve its first profit target, which was 50 percent of the range of the first bar. On day number three a trigger occurred on the second bar and prices then quickly went on to achieve all profit targets before the end of the day.

Figure 8.6 shows two consecutive 30 MBO trades, each of which triggered and achieved profit targets. On the first day shown (September 3, 2008) a trigger occurred in bar number five, but the trade was not profitable. Note that if a trader had bought early in

FIGURE 8.5

Three consecutive 30 MBO Trades, 8/27/08

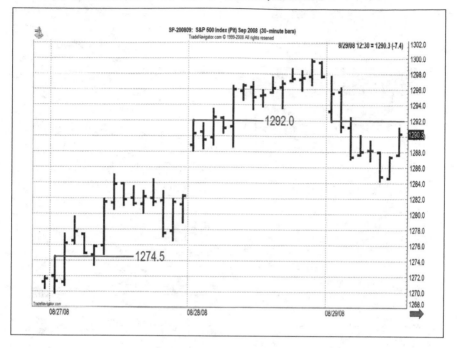

the day, when prices penetrated the first bar high but did not close above it, it would have been two losses rather than just one. On the next day, the losses from the previous day were easily compensated for and exceeded by good profits, which points out the importance of consistency in following this or any other trading methodology.

Figure 8.7 shows how the 30 MBO performed during the stock market crash of 1987. It is fascinating and noteworthy to observe how a short-sale trigger occurred early in the day and how follow through on the downside on the last position would have produced the largest profit.

Figure 8.8 shows three consecutive 30 MBO trades. On the first day (May 23, 2012) the trigger occurred at the end of the second bar, after which prices went on to achieve all profit targets and to reverse to later in the day. Although profitable, this trade would have been too late to enter because 30 MBO trades that do not trigger prior to the last hour and a half of trading should not be taken. On

FIGURE 8.6

Two consecutive 30 MBO trades, 9/03/08

FIGURE 8.7

30 MBO trade during stock market crash '87

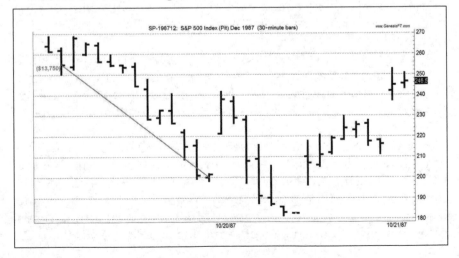

FIGURE 8.8

Three consecutive MBO trades, 5/23/12

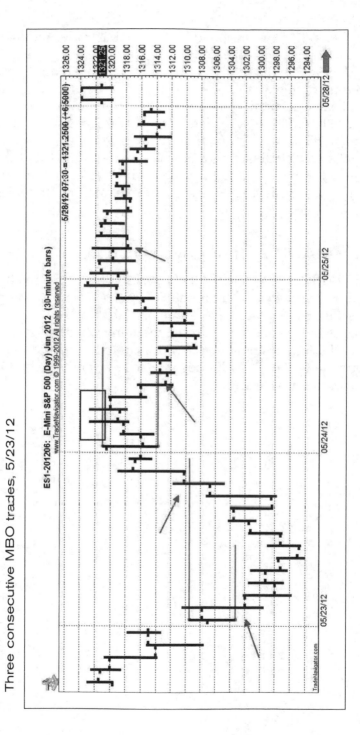

ES1-201206: E-Mini S&P 500 (Day) Jun 2012 (30-minute bars)
www.TradeNavigator.com © 1999-2012 All rights reserved

May 24 a sell trigger resulted in a profitable trade, and the 30 MBO on May 25 also was profitable.

Figure 8.9 illustrates a losing day on the 30 MBO. On the second bar trigger was established in the long trade but would not have been closed out until the second arrow toward the end of the day at a loss. This was too late in the day to go short for a short-sell trade, so the day ended with one loss.

Figure 8.10 illustrates a perfect day for the 30 MBO. A sell was triggered in bar number four, after which prices continued lower, meeting all profit targets and profit-maximizing strategies by the end of the day.

SUMMARY AND CONCLUSION

The 30 MBO is a powerful but not perfect day trading methodology for those who wish to trade the E-Mini S&P futures contract. The rules are clear and objective. Remember that the key to success with the 30 MBO is consistency; resist the temptation to give up on the method after a losing trade. If you want to be very conservative in starting to use the 30 MBO, begin to do so after the 30 MBO has had three consecutive losses.

FIGURE 8.9

30 MBO loss

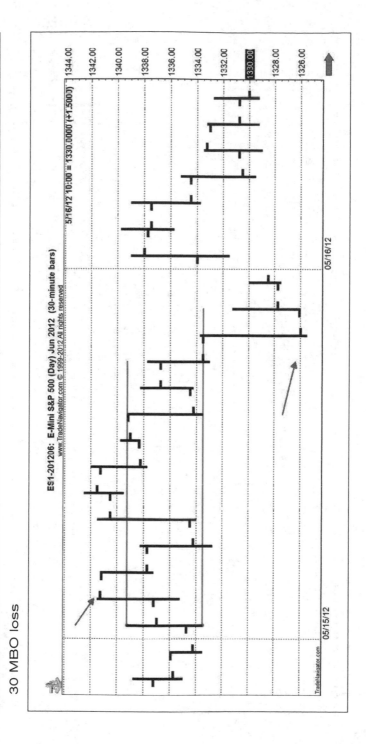

ES1-201206: E-Mini S&P 500 (Day) Jun 2012 (30-minute bars)
www.TradeNavigator.com © 1999-2012 All rights reserved

5/16/12 10:00 = 1330.0000 (+1.5000)

FIGURE 8.10

30 MBO perfect day

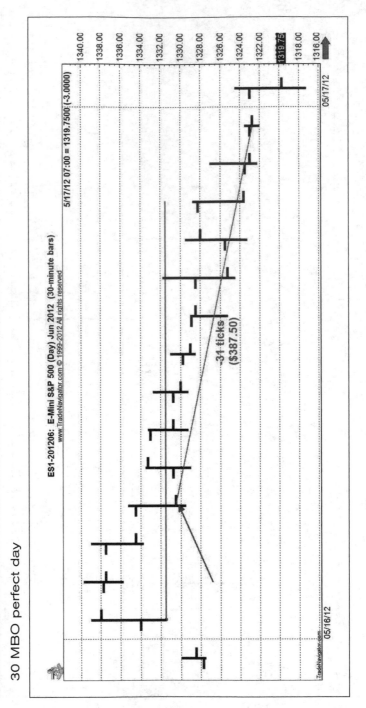

ES1-201206: E-Mini S&P 500 (Day) Jun 2012 (30-minute bars)
www.TradeNavigator.com © 1999-2012 All rights reserved

5/17/12 07:00 = 1319.7500 (-3.0000)

-31 ticks
($387.50)

CHAPTER 9

What Not to Do

Most of this book is dedicated to providing you with specific information on how to day trade. I have spent considerable time and effort to provide you with examples of specific indicators, setups, triggers, and follow throughs. There is even more information coming in subsequent chapters. I have provided lists of methods and procedures that facilitate success. I may have been redundant in sharing with you what, based on my own experience, can take you to a higher level in trading.

Knowing what to do is very important, but knowing what *not* to do is also important. There are literally thousands of mistakes you can make. Every mistake has the potential to be costly and, in the worst case, wipe out your entire account. Although there are very few things you can do that are right, there are many things you can do that are wrong. In this chapter I will give you some specific guidelines as to what I consider to be wrong when it comes to trading—behaviors and procedures that negatively correlate with success. Naturally, there will be those who disagree with my guidelines. You must decide for yourself. Consider what you read in this chapter in the context of what you have experienced and make your own decisions accordingly.

If you take a course on trading, whether in college, on the Internet, or in the form of a live seminar or webinar, your instructor(s) will give you information that may or may not be specific or fully objective. As I've noted throughout this book, information that requires interpretation is often useless and potentially harmful because it depends upon the user to interpret its meaning as well as its application. I have emphasized the importance of objectivity. Clearly we know that being objective facilitates success. The list of profitable procedures and behaviors is relatively short. I have already briefly discussed some of the behaviors and procedures that in my experience limit success or might even guarantee failure. In providing you with my "do not do" list, I am fully aware that I may make a few more enemies in the trading world. People in this business tend to get very possessive about their pet methods and indicators, often clinging to them ferociously whether or not they are profitable. I can only tell you what has and has not worked for me. Try my suggestions on for size. At least give them a fair test.

DO NOT MIX TIME FRAMES

As you well know, a day trade is a trade in to which you enter and exit during the trading day. This very broad definition covers a multitude of sins. Day traders come in all shapes, sizes, colors, and time frames. By this I mean that some traders will enter a day trade using a 30-minute chart and then exit the day trade using a one-minute chart. There are many possible combinations of time frames, but I urge you to use this combination judiciously; better yet, avoid it altogether. Based on my experience, I can tell you that the time frame that gets you in should be the time frame that gets you out. If you decide to mix time frames, do so only once you have verified and back tested your procedures. In other words, if you trade my methods using a 10-minute chart for entry and exit positions using a two-minute chart, make certain ahead of time that this is a profitable procedure. I have seen a number of trading methods that use a triple time frame approach. They will only enter or exit trades if several time frames are pointing in the right direction. Though you should decide for yourself, I have found this approach to be confusing and unprofitable.

AVOID INDICATORS THAT HAVE UPPER AND LOWER LIMITS

Indicators that have uppers and lowers give numerous false signals, particularly when used in the "overbought" and "oversold" approach. Let me give you a specific example: The popular indicator RSI (relative strength index), as developed by J. Welles Wilder, has an upper limit of 100 and a lower limit of zero. Traders frequently use RSI as an overbought or oversold indicator. When RSI goes above 75, it supposedly precedes a top in prices, whereas falling below 25 supposedly precedes a bottom in prices. I have found this to be incorrect. Because RSI and indicators of a similar nature can only go to zero as the lower limit and 100 as the upper limit, it is possible for RSI to drop to near zero while prices continue to go down. It is possible for RSI to approach 100 while prices continue to move higher. The trader who mistakenly believes that the underlying market is going to top because RSI is "too high" will often be incorrect, and large losses may ensue.

The stochastic indicator, as developed by George Lane, has similar problems and should be avoided for the overbought or oversold condition. Having said that, I will add the caveat that there are ways in which both indicators can be used successfully but not purely in the overbought or oversold sense. One way to overcome the problem is to wait until these indicators become overbought and then turn lower, indicating that the underlying market has turned lower.

In general, however, I believe there are much better ways of determining overbought and oversold conditions using such indicators as momentum, rate of change, momentum and its moving average, and the relationship between opening and closing prices.

DO NOT SET A DAILY DOLLAR PROFIT GOAL

I've often heard newcomers say that they want to make $500 a day, and that once they've reached their target their day is done. I believe setting a daily goal for your day trading profits is utterly absurd. Your goal should be to make as much money as you possibly can each day, and you shouldn't quit when you've reached a certain dollar amount. Clearly, setting such goals limits your potential profit. On the other hand, deciding on a maximum dollar loss per day would be reasonable.

DO NOT LISTEN TO THE EXPERTS

In this age of instant communication and cable news channels such as CNBC, there is a wealth of information available to all traders. Add into the mix the constant stream of trading recommendations and news that comes to you via the Internet, and you have a recipe for disaster. I have made my best decisions when trading in isolation. I do everything I can to shut out the news and, at the very minimum, avoid trading on the news. There is one notable exception to this approach, which is what I call the media trade. This has been described in one of my previous books, *The Compleat Day Trader, 2nd Edition*.

DO NOT BELIEVE THAT MORE IS MORE

The popular misconceptions that more information is better than less, a bigger and better computer is better than a smaller one, more trading will make you more money, and the more markets you look at the more money will make are not true. If you are a high-frequency trader, by which I mean you trade in a time frame of milliseconds with exceptionally large positions, all of the above may be true. However, the high-frequency approach is not for individuals who are incapable of trading in ultra large positions in ultrashort time frames. Many times less is more.

DO NOT MICROMANAGE POSITIONS

By this I mean avoiding living and dying with every price during the day. Once you have set your plan and entered a trade, determine your exit strategy and stay with it as closely as you can. Should you find that you are getting out repeatedly with much smaller profits than originally planned and that eventual prices in most cases do go to your targets, you are micromanaging your trades and are most likely making emotionally based decisions as opposed to technically based ones. Micromanaging trades will often get you into trouble or, worse, cause you to take losses when you should be taking profits.

DO NOT BEAT THE BUSHES TO FIND TRADES

All too often traders get the feeling they should be doing more trades. On a day on which very few opportunities present themselves, some traders begin searching frantically for things to do. Many times the opportunities that present themselves are not the best ones. Your goal is to make trades based on quality as opposed to quantity. Take your time, and wait for the best opportunities rather than trading because you feel you should be doing *something*.

DO NOT INCREASE POSITION SIZE PREMATURELY

After a winning streak, some traders will begin to suffer from the "King Kong complex." They begin to feel that they are invulnerable, that they have really learned how to trade, that they are fantastic traders, and therefore that they should be trading larger positions. That is not the way to determine when to increase position size. I am by my very nature a conservative trader, which is one of the reasons I'm still around after 40-plus years. My rule of thumb is to increase my position size after I have doubled my account. You may feel this is overly conservative, but I have seen too many cases in which traders have increased their position size too quickly and have in the long run given back all the money they've made plus more.

DO NOT IGNORE YOUR LOSSES AND TURN THEM INTO INVESTMENTS

The day trade is a day trade is a day trade. Win, lose, or draw, a day trade must be ended by the end of the day. Too many traders, myself included, have carried losing trades to the next day in the hope that they will not have to take a loss on them. Such trades have an uncanny way of getting worse rather than better. Some of my worst losses have happened that way. The sad part of this is that they were more often than not larger losses than they should have been.

DO NOT ALLOW YOUR DAY TRADE MENTALITY TO INFLUENCE YOUR INVESTMENT MENTALITY

As a day trader, you will be inclined to take profits quickly because you need to be out of trades by the end of the day. You will not want to let profitable opportunities slip away from you to become losses. Once you have become a veteran of many day trades and have mastered your skill as a day trader, you may find your approach toward investments has been affected adversely, applying the same urgency to take profits on investments as opposed to allowing them to do what they were originally intended to do: make money over the long run. You need to be especially careful not to let your short-term thinking become part of your intermediate- to longer-term thinking. Finally, as your short-term goals are constantly being rewarded, you will see opportunities to take quick profits all around you. It will become increasingly difficult for you to see investments in their proper light, and you must therefore be very cautious about the potential spillover from one point of view and approach to the other.

DO NOT BELIEVE WHAT YOU ARE TOLD

There is so much bad information these days and so many individuals out there who want to sell you the Brooklyn Bridge that it becomes difficult to discern the real from the phony. Most of the people who make fantastic claims about what you will get when you buy their system or use their method are doing so either based on cherry-picked or overly optimized results. I am not claiming that everything out there is fake, but you are ultimately responsible for doing your own due diligence on what is advertised. Whether this applies to anything I tell you or anything anyone else tells you, take your time, examine what is being told, try it out for yourself on hypothetical trades, and give yourself sufficient time to evaluate whether the approach is right for you. Then decide whether you will put real money to work on it.

WATCH OUT FOR TRACK RECORDS

A track record is most often hypothetical. A track record that is real may not necessarily reflect what you as an individual can achieve. You may not be able to do the things the individual who developed the track record can because you may not have enough money, enough time, or enough discipline to achieve the same results. Remember also that track records are based on perfect situations. I have explained earlier that some aspects of day trading are extremely difficult to mechanize in a fully computerized trading system because exit strategies are, in my view, subject to change based on market conditions. Entry strategies can be totally mechanical, but exit strategies can't.

DO NOT TRY TO TRADE THE WORLD

You are far better off specializing in several methods and/or markets and time frames as opposed to trying to do everything. Trading is all about consistency. If you jump from one stock to another or from one futures market or Forex market to another, taking trades randomly or on a whim, you will completely miss the regularity or patterns that occur in these markets. Although it may be unexciting, the best thing you can do is to specialize in certain markets and certain methods and to turn all cranks at once to get the music of profits.

DO NOT COMPARE YOUR PERFORMANCE TO ANYONE ELSE'S

There will always be someone who is doing better than you, or at least they will say so. There will always be statistics about how well hedge funds or managed accounts are doing. There will always be someone out there who can make you feel bad or inadequate or incompetent or unequipped to be successful. You can beat yourself up about it, or you can compare yourself only with your performance. Are you doing better or worse than you did last month, last year, or last week? Are you improving? Are you feeling competent in your skills? Does your bottom-line profit reflect a growing trend?

Are you making the same mistakes repeatedly? Are you learning from your mistakes? These are the questions you should be asking and answering, and the comparisons you make should be only with your own progress as opposed to what you see or hear or read about other traders.

CONCLUSION

Given enough time I could most likely expand this chapter to five times its length by continuing to share with you what I have learned about what not to do in day trading. The items cited are a good start to understanding the pitfalls and avoiding them. I encourage you to make your own list based on what has worked for you and what you have seen in your own behavior.

CHAPTER 10

Risk, Reward, and Profit-Maximizing Strategies

While many traders understand the importance of managing risk through the use of stop losses and trailing stop losses, relatively few traders have developed profit-maximizing strategies. My experience as a trader for over 40 years has led me to a number of valid and persistent conclusions that have served me well and that I believe can do the same for you. But my conclusions and recommendations will be to no avail unless they are implemented consistently, aggressively, and persistently. My suggested strategies must be more than just words on a piece of paper or a computer screen. The successful trader takes action. The losing trader pays lip service to highly valid concepts and procedures.

Here is my list of the most important issues and obstacles you will have to confront, as well as some suggested solutions.

PREDETERMINED STOP LOSS AND FIRST PROFIT TARGET

Every trade you make must have a predetermined stop loss, as well as a predetermined first profit target. Unless this requirement is met before any trades are made, you are inviting failure, whether you believe that to be true or not. Hundreds of thousands, if not more, have come to the day trading game convinced they are able to determine probable price direction intuitively or observation-ally, simply by looking at a price chart or listening to the news. I have not met any traders who can consistently achieve this goal without clear, specific, predetermined, and operational stop loss and profit target rules. But that is only the first step. These specific stop loss and profit target rules must be objective as well as consistently applied. Where will these numbers come from? From methodologies such as the ones described in this book. If you recall the 30-minute breakout method discussed in Chapter 8, you know that there is a specific stop loss as well as a specific profit target for every trade. By now this fact should be self-evident. If it is not—if you still believe you can observe or interpret your way to trading success— I respectfully submit to you that you are wrong, and if you are right, your odds of having achieved lasting success using your intuition will be about the same as your odds of winning the lottery.

OBJECTIVE PROCEDURE

The stop loss and profit target must be based on an objective pro-cedure such as a system, average profit per move, projected price pattern, or objective forecast of price trends. Clearly this relates to what has already been discussed above, and I refer you to all the methods discussed in this book for details of how such numbers are derived. If you are one of the unfortunate many who have been exposed to the type of vague, useless, and unprofitable "techniques" being marketed—some at a hefty price—on the Internet, you know exactly what I mean. I caution and urge you to stay away from any-thing and everything relating to day trading (or, for that matter, any other type of trading) that is not 100 percent objective. I will be slightly flexible and suggest that if you can achieve 90 percent objectivity, you are still doing quite well, but you have not gone the full distance and are therefore not doing yourself a favor but rather exposing yourself to unnecessary losses.

UNDERSTAND THE UNDERLYING SYSTEM

The stop loss for each trade must be a function of the underlying system, not just a function of what you can afford to risk. Every objective trading methodology and system contains information on dollar risk, stop losses, or both. If it does not, it is clearly not a system or a strategy. Some people believe that they can day trade S&P futures with a $200 stop loss. Without a doubt the markets are not sensitive to, nor do they care about, how much you can afford to risk. A market will do what it does and establish its level of volatility. In most cases market volatility, as defined by the price swing from high to low on any given day, will be relatively stable. There are, however, occasions on which market volatility increases dramatically as a function of underlying fundamentals or news. All active trading systems will have rules for dealing with such behavior.

Either the rules will be in the form of "Do not risk more than X dollars on any trade" or they will automatically adjust their suggested stop loss based on measures of volatility. To risk $300 on a day trade in a market that regularly moves $1200 from high to low is absurd, an invitation to lose money. The good news about using stop losses that are very small is that you will not lose very much. The bad news is that you will lose every time! As an example, consider the following series of system test results.

Tables 10.1 through 10.6 show the same trading strategy with different stop loss amounts. Note the significant improvement in performance as the size of the stop loss increases. Note also that the stop loss size eventually reaches a point of diminishing returns, at which an increase in the stop loss no longer improves performance commensurately. It is important to remember that up to a given point, the larger your stop loss, the better will your performance. This fact flies in the face of the commonly held belief that a small stop loss will protect you from losing too much money.

MULTIPLE POSITIONS

Trading in multiple positions allows you the flexibility of taking some profits, riding in profits, and holding some profits for the anticipated large move. Most new traders are one-lot traders, meaning they trade in units of 100 shares or one futures contract. They tend to get out of their 100 shares or one futures contract a predetermined profit target; therefore they more often than not miss the big move. By having more than one unit or lot, you put

TABLE 10.1

Trading strategy history with $500 stop loss

Summary—All Trades			
Overall			
Total Net Profit:	$34,106	Profit Factor ($Wins/$Losses):	**1.44**
Total Trades:	273	Winning Percentage:	45.8%
Average Trade:	$125	Payout Ratio (Avg Win/Avg Loss):	1.70
Max Closed-out Drawdown:	**−$5,141**	CPC Index (PF x Win% x PR):	1.12
Max Intraday Drawdown:	**−$5,150**	Expectancy (Avg Trade/Avg Loss):	23.74%
Account Size Required:	$10,550	Return Pct:	**323.3%**
Open Equity:	$0	Kelly Pct (Avg Trade/Avg Win):	13.94%
Percent in the Market:	5.4%	Optimal f:	0.36
Avg # of Bars in Trade:	0.56	Z-Score (W/L Predictability):	−0.6
Avg # of Trades per Year:	27.4	Current Streak:	3 Losses

Monthly Profit Analysis			
Average Monthly Profit:	$282	Monthly Sharpe Ratio:	0.20
Std Dev of Monthly Profits:	$1,320	Annualized Sharpe Ratio:	0.70
		Calmar Ratio:	0.66

Winning Trades		**Losing Trades**	
Total Winners:	125	Total Losers:	148
Gross Profit:	$111,988	Gross Loss:	**−$77,882**
Average Win:	$896	Average Loss:	**−$526**
Largest Win:	$4,041	Largest Loss:	**−$1,847**
Largest Drawdown in Win:	**−$484**	Largest Peak in Loss:	$1,141
Avg Drawdown in Win:	**−$37**	Avg Peak in Loss:	$49
Avg Run Up in Win:	$1,156	Avg Run Up in Loss:	$49
Avg Run Down in Win:	**−$37**	Avg Run Down in Loss:	**−$526**
Most Consec Wins:	6	Most Consec Losses:	8
Avg # of Consec Wins:	1.92	Avg # of Consec Losses:	2.24
Avg # of Bars in Wins:	1.03	Avg # of Bars in Losses:	0.16

TABLE 10.2

Trading strategy history with $1000 stop loss

Summary—All Trades			
Overall			
Total Net Profit:	$28,393	Profit Factor ($Wins/$Losses):	**1.25**
Total Trades:	273	Winning Percentage:	60.4%
Average Trade:	$104	Payout Ratio (Avg Win/Avg Loss):	0.82
Max Closed-out Drawdown:	**-$8,792**	CPC Index (PF x Win% x PR):	0.62
Max Intraday Drawdown:	**-$8,801**	Expectancy (Avg Trade/Avg Loss):	9.98%
Account Size Required:	$14,201	Return Pct:	**199.9%**
Open Equity:	$0	Kelly Pct (Avg Trade/Avg Win):	12.18%
Percent in the Market:	9.1%	Optimal f:	0.22
Avg # of Bars in Trade:	0.93	Z-Score (W/L Predictability):	-1.3
Avg # of Trades per Year:	27.4	Current Streak:	3 Losses

Monthly Profit Analysis			
Average Monthly Profit:	$235	Monthly Sharpe Ratio:	0.13
Std Dev of Monthly Profits:	$1,695	Annualized Sharpe Ratio:	0.44
		Calmar Ratio:	0.32

Winning Trades		Losing Trades	
Total Winners:	165	Total Losers:	108
Gross Profit:	$140,915	Gross Loss:	**-$112,522**
Average Win:	$854	Average Loss:	**-$1,042**
Largest Win:	$4,041	Largest Loss:	**-$2,409**
Largest Drawdown in Win:	**-$959**	Largest Peak in Loss:	$1,141
Avg Drawdown in Win:	**-$96**	Avg Peak in Loss:	$153
Avg Run Up in Win:	$1,101	Avg Run Up in Loss:	$153
Avg Run Down in Win:	**-$96**	Avg Run Down in Loss:	**-$1,042**
Most Consec Wins:	14	Most Consec Losses:	7
Avg # of Consec Wins:	2.75	Avg # of Consec Losses:	1.77
Avg # of Bars in Wins:	1.18	Avg # of Bars in Losses:	0.56

TABLE 10.3

Trading strategy history with $1500 stop loss

Summary—All Trades			
Overall			
Total Net Profit:	$46,543	Profit Factor ($Wins/$Losses):	**1.39**
Total Trades:	273	Winning Percentage:	71.4%
Average Trade:	$170	Payout Ratio (Avg Win/Avg Loss):	0.55
Max Closed-out Drawdown:	**−$9,830**	CPC Index (PF x Win% x PR):	0.55
Max Intraday Drawdown:	**−$9,913**	Expectancy (Avg Trade/Avg Loss):	11.06%
Account Size Required:	$15,313	Return Pct:	**304.0%**
Open Equity:	$0	Kelly Pct (Avg Trade/Avg Win):	19.94%
Percent in the Market:	13.0%	Optimal f:	0.31
Avg # of Bars in Trade:	1.34	Z-Score (W/L Predictability):	−2.5
Avg # of Trades per Year:	27.4	Current Streak:	3 Losses
Monthly Profit Analysis			
Average Monthly Profit:	$385	Monthly Sharpe Ratio:	0.19
Std Dev of Monthly Profits:	$1,950	Annualized Sharpe Ratio:	0.64
		Calmar Ratio:	0.47
Winning Trades		**Losing Trades**	
Total Winners:	195	Total Losers:	78
Gross Profit:	$166,758	Gross Loss:	**−$120,215**
Average Win:	$855	Average Loss:	**−$1,541**
Largest Win:	$4,041	Largest Loss:	**−$2,859**
Largest Drawdown in Win:	**−$1,459**	Largest Peak in Loss:	$3,679
Avg Drawdown in Win:	**−$230**	Avg Peak in Loss:	$259
Avg Run Up in Win:	$1,118	Avg Run Up in Loss:	$259
Avg Run Down in Win:	**−$230**	Avg Run Down in Loss:	**−$1,543**
Most Consec Wins:	18	Most Consec Losses:	4
Avg # of Consec Wins:	4.15	Avg # of Consec Losses:	1.63
Avg # of Bars in Wins:	1.46	Avg # of Bars in Losses:	1.04

TABLE 10.4

Trading strategy history with $2500 stop loss

Summary—All Trades			
Overall			
Total Net Profit:	$52,836	Profit Factor ($Wins/$Losses):	**1.41**
Total Trades:	271	Winning Percentage:	80.8%
Average Trade:	$195	Payout Ratio (Avg Win/Avg Loss):	0.33
Max Closed-out Drawdown:	–$16,308	CPC Index (PF x Win% x PR):	0.38
Max Intraday Drawdown:	–$16,317	Expectancy (Avg Trade/Avg Loss):	7.81%
Account Size Required:	$21,717	Return Pct:	**243.3%**
Open Equity:	**–$484**	Kelly Pct (Avg Trade/Avg Win):	23.37%
Percent in the Market:	20.0%	Optimal f:	0.26
Avg # of Bars in Trade:	2.07	Z-Score (W/L Predictability):	–2.3
Avg # of Trades per Year:	27.2	Current Streak:	2 Losses
Monthly Profit Analysis			
Average Monthly Profit:	$440	Monthly Sharpe Ratio:	0.17
Std Dev of Monthly Profits:	$2,346	Annualized Sharpe Ratio:	0.60
		Calmar Ratio:	0.32
Winning Trades		**Losing Trades**	
Total Winners:	219	Total Losers:	52
Gross Profit:	$182,692	Gross Loss:	–$129,856
Average Win:	$834	Average Loss:	–$2,497
Largest Win:	$4,041	Largest Loss:	–$3,234
Largest Drawdown in Win:	–$2,459	Largest Peak in Loss:	$3,679
Avg Drawdown in Win:	–$415	Avg Peak in Loss:	$428
Avg Run Up in Win:	$1,102	Avg Run Up in Loss:	$428
Avg Run Down in Win:	–$415	Avg Run Down in Loss:	–$2,501
Most Consec Wins:	19	Most Consec Losses:	3
Avg # of Consec Wins:	6.08	Avg # of Consec Losses:	1.41
Avg # of Bars in Wins:	1.89	Avg # of Bars in Losses:	2.83

TABLE 10.5

Trading strategy history with $4000 stop loss

Summary—All Trades
Overall

Total Net Profit:	$69,024	Profit Factor ($Wins/$Losses):	**1.54**
Total Trades:	271	Winning Percentage:	86.0%
Average Trade:	$255	Payout Ratio (Avg Win/Avg Loss):	0.25
Max Closed-out Drawdown:	**−$15,612**	CPC Index (PF x Win% x PR):	0.33
Max Intraday Drawdown:	**−$15,612**	Expecta.ncy (Avg Trade/Avg Loss):	7.62%
Account Size Required:	$21,012	Return Pct:	**328.5%**
Open Equity:	**−$559**	Kelly Pct (Avg Trade/Avg Win):	30.26%
Percent in the Market:	27.6%	Optimal f:	0.34
Avg # of Bars in Trade:	2.87	Z-Score (W/L Predictability):	−1.0
Avg # of Trades per Year:	27.2	Current Streak:	2 Losses

Monthly Profit Analysis

Average Monthly Profit:	$575	Monthly Sharpe Ratio:	0.22
Std Dev of Monthly Profits:	$2,451	Annualized Sharpe Ratio:	0.77
		Calmar Ratio:	0.44

Winning Trades		Losing Trades	
Total Winners:	233	Total Losers:	38
Gross Profit:	$196,103	Gross Loss:	**−$127,080**
Average Win:	$842	Average Loss:	**−$3,344**
Largest Win:	$4,041	Largest Loss:	**−$4,547**
Largest Drawdown in Win:	**−$3,922**	Largest Peak in Loss:	$1,316
Avg Drawdown in Win:	**−$575**	Avg Peak in Loss:	$399
Avg Run Up in Win:	$1,129	Avg Run Up in Loss:	$399
Avg Run Down in Win:	**−$575**	Avg Run Down in Loss:	**−$3,576**
Most Consec Wins:	22	Most Consec Losses:	3
Avg # of Consec Wins:	7.52	Avg # of Consec Losses:	1.23
Avg # of Bars in Wins:	2.35	Avg # of Bars in Losses:	6.08

TABLE 10.6

Trading strategy history with no stop loss

Summary—All Trades			
Overall			
Total Net Profit:	$75,026	Profit Factor ($Wins/$Losses):	**1.60**
Total Trades:	268	Winning Percentage:	84.7%
Average Trade:	$280	Payout Ratio (Avg Win/Avg Loss):	0.29
Max Closed-out Drawdown:	−$37,453	CPC Index (PF x Win% x PR):	0.39
Max Intraday Drawdown:	−$37,453	Expectancy (Avg Trade/Avg Loss):	9.12%
Account Size Required:	$42,853	Return Pct:	**175.1%**
Open Equity:	−$3,656	Kelly Pct (Avg Trade/Avg Win):	31.62%
Percent in the Market:	42.8%	Optimal f:	0.61
Avg # of Bars in Trade:	4.49	Z-Score (W/L Predictability):	−3.8
Avg # of Trades per Year:	26.9	Current Streak:	1 Loss

Monthly Profit Analysis			
Average Monthly Profit:	$625	Monthly Sharpe Ratio:	0.17
Std Dev of Monthly Profits:	$3,246	Annualized Sharpe Ratio:	0.60
		Calmar Ratio:	0.20

Winning Trades		**Losing Trades**	
Total Winners:	227	Total Losers:	41
Gross Profit:	$200,945	Gross Loss:	**−$125,919**
Average Win:	$885	Average Loss:	**−$3,071**
Largest Win:	$4,041	Largest Loss:	**−$12,147**
Largest Drawdown in Win:	**−$5,822**	Largest Peak in Loss:	$4,129
Avg Drawdown in Win:	**−$658**	Avg Peak in Loss:	$765
Avg Run Up in Win:	$1,216	Avg Run Up in Loss:	$765
Avg Run Down in Win:	**−$658**	Avg Run Down in Loss:	**−$4,732**
Most Consec Wins:	21	Most Consec Losses:	7
Avg # of Consec Wins:	8.41	Avg # of Consec Losses:	1.52
Avg # of Bars in Wins:	2.71	Avg # of Bars in Losses:	14.34

yourself in the position of potentially being in the market when the big move comes. Success at day trading is all about catching the big move. You can't catch the big move unless you have more than one position or you have a methodology by which you can ride your one position for the big move. Granted the big move may not come, but at least you have a "free trade" with the stop loss at breakeven in the event that there is a large move in your favor.

BIG MONEY IS MADE IN THE BIG MOVE

It is important to remember that 80 to 90 percent of your money is going to be made on 10 to 20 percent of your trades. The big money is made in the big move. This is just another way of saying that your bottom line will depend upon having captured large trades. When you day trade you are forced to exit by the end of the day, win, lose, or draw. Many large moves happen overnight, which means that as a day trader you may miss them. This does not change the fact that many large moves occur within the time frame of the day. In order to achieve the goal of capturing big moves, you will need to have a profit-maximizing strategy that retains part of your position beyond any profit target during the day but exits either at a predetermined "maximum profit" using a trailing stop procedure or exits at the end of the day. There are several techniques you can use as a day trader to capture a large move when it happens. This is so important that I have devoted Chapter 11 to several objective ways in which to capture the big move.

FIGHT TEMPTATION

The day trader must always fight the temptation to hold a trade beyond the end of the day, either hoping that losing trade will become profitable or that a profitable trade will become even more profitable. To do so defeats the purpose of day trading. I have been guilty of doing that too many times myself. The good news is that I make that mistake less frequently as time goes on. I firmly believe that a trade entered as a day trade must be closed out as a day trade and that there should be very few exceptions to that rule. In Chapter 11 I discuss several of these exceptions as part of my profit-maximizing strategy suggestions. Note that holding a trade beyond the end of the day could also affect your broker's margin requirement, in as much as day trades in some markets qualify for day trade margins that are considerably lower than full margin. (i.e. futures)

POSITION COMMITMENT

One of the most difficult issues that confront day traders, whether in stocks, Forex, or commodities, is how much of their account should be committed to positions and, secondarily, how large their positions should be. As a day trader you must survive the game long enough to capture the winning trades when they come. The only way you can do that is by limiting your risk. The only way to limit risk is to determine what percentage of your account should be risked on any given trade. The rule of thumb here is very simple. In stocks I suggest 5 percent of your account size. In futures I suggest 3 percent.

Consider the following example: You have a $50,000 day trading account. There is a day trade you would like to make based on a signal. The stock is trading at $50 a share. The risk is $3 a share. If you buy 100 shares and you are wrong, you lose $300. If you buy 300 shares and you are wrong, you lose $900. Let's make this easier and round the $900 to $1,000 to account for commissions and poor price execution. You are now risking $1,000 of your $50,000 account. A 10 percent risk of your account would be $5,000. A 1 percent risk would be $500; a 5 percent risk of your account size, as suggested, would be $2,500. If you trade 600 shares of the stock and you are wrong, you're risk would be $2,000. This would be an acceptable trade; it comes in at under your $2,500 maximum risk and also allows you to trade multiple positions. My suggestion would be that you commit 75 percent of your total account equity to trades at one time and that you risk 5 percent, as indicated, for any one position. While some more conservative traders would find my suggestions too liberal, I believe this formula will work. But only you can determine what is right for your account, risk tolerance, and psychology. You must walk that fine line between risking too much and not risking enough. Risking too much can kick you out of the game, but not risking enough will keep you from making money. My guidelines, I hope, will help you make the decision.

STAY FOCUSED

Closely related to all of the issues already discussed is the idea of focus—doing a few things well, as opposed to many things poorly. Profitable day trading requires considerable focus, including attention to detail as well as attention to specific methods and markets. The day trader must frequently make choices as to which method or methods to employ. No matter how new you are to the game of day trading, you will know that there are literally hundreds of trading methods available to you. In order to find the one that is right for you, you will need to research, study, and learn. Some of the best day traders I know focus on only one market using one method, and they learn how to use that method extremely well.

I have advised you that in day trading less is more. If you are a futures trader, you will only have relatively few markets from which to choose your candidates for day trades. These include some of the currencies, Treasury bond futures, crude oil futures, and S&P futures. In stocks you have many from which to choose. I urge you to develop a list or stable of candidates from which you will day trade consistently. Make your determination on the liquidity—trading volume—as well as the potential size of the move each day. A stock or commodity market that makes very small intraday moves will not be a good candidate for your day-trading venture.

KNOW WHEN TO INCREASE THE SIZE OF YOUR TRADING

Another critically important issue for the day trader is when to increase the size of your trading. I have given you a few suggestions as to how this might be done and indicated that there are specific formulae that can tell you when to increase position size (detailed information about the Kelly formula can be found online

FIGURE 10.1

Trading system X history using one futures contract per signal

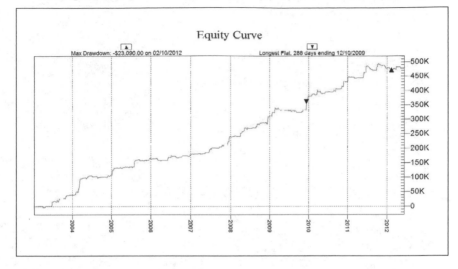

at http://en.wikipedia.org/wiki/Kelly_criterion). You must know not only when to increase the size of your position but also when to decrease it. Some software programs that are part of charting packages, as well as some independent programs, can help you determine objective answers to these questions. As an example, consider the performance track record of a particular system using one futures contract per trade, which will represent the performance of trading one contract each time, no matter how well or how poorly the system performed. Figure 10.1 shows the chart history of this system.

Now add a specific money management system to the methodology, which allows more or fewer contracts to be traded based on system performance, comparing the result again, as shown in Figure 10.2.

ACCOUNT SIZE

Finally, let's consider the critically important issue of account size. Many day traders believe they can be successful in this game by beginning with a small amount of capital. Over the years the

FIGURE 10.2

System X history using multiple futures contracts based on
the Kelly formula

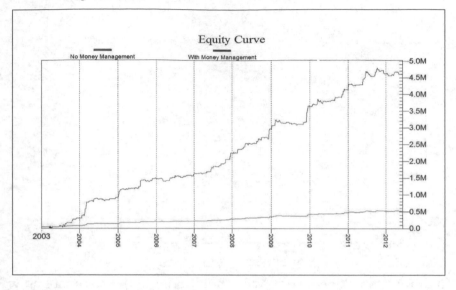

definition of a "small amount of capital" has changed dramatically not only as a result of increased market volatility but also
as a result of increased prices and broker requirements for more
margin due to increased prices and volatility. It is possible that by
the time you read this book, any suggestion(s) I could give you in
terms of dollars for a starting account may have changed.

Furthermore, reasonable starting amounts for stock trading,
futures trading, options trading, and Forex trading vary substan-
tially. Here are some general guidelines for stocks, futures, and/or
options:

1. Start with pure risk capital. In other words, start with money
   you can afford to lose.

2. Be prepared to suffer 8 consecutive losses and still have
   sufficient capital to continue your trading.

3. Have sufficient capital to trade at least 3 units (i.e., 300 shares,
   3 futures contracts, 3 options) in at least 5 uncorrelated
   markets or stocks.

CHAPTER 11

What You Will Need to Facilitate Success

Success as a day trader will not be found or achieved by reading a book, participating in a seminar, or using a particular software program. There are literally thousands of day trading methods that purport to help you to be profitable. There are many self-proclaimed gurus in the trading business who would have you follow their lead down the road to success. Be careful what you believe, be careful what you tell yourself, and be careful what you do. The simple fact of the matter is that traders all over the world struggle every day, but very few actually achieve success. There are many reasons why it is so difficult to achieve success as a day trader, or trading in any time frame, for that matter. As I have stated, there are many things you can do wrong in the markets but relatively few things you can do right. Indeed I could repeat the litany of potential errors, but knowing what not to do is less than half of the equation to success. You need to know what to do that's right; otherwise nothing will work for you.

Traders often confuse method and system with procedure and implementation. Just as you cannot learn to ride a bicycle by reading a book, you cannot achieve success as a day trader by reading a book or taking a course. Once you have learned some potentially profitable day trading approaches, you need to implement those approaches flawlessly with the correct sequence or procedure if you are to be successful. Over time and with experience, every trader can develop her own style. The style a day trader develops is not only a function of the methods she uses, the risk capital she has available, the risk level she wants to assume, the frequency of her trading signals, and her risk-management procedures but also a function of her personality. That is why I have found that if I teach exactly the same day trading method to 10 people, the trading results easily can vary from one trader to the next. In fact the differences can be so extreme that one trader may show profits while another shows losses using—or supposedly using—exactly the same method. The factors that account for the differences are procedure, implementation, and the ability to take risk and maximize profits. Somewhere during the transition from recognizing a trading signal to implementing and exiting a trade things may go astray.

In this chapter I explore and suggest some ideas that will help you avoid the behavioral pitfalls of day trading while adopting and maximizing the behavioral procedures for facilitating profits and making them grow. Every suggestion I offer here has come from my personal experiences as a trader, as well as my observations of the many traders I have personally coached over the years.

DAILY PROCEDURE

The first and possibly most important thing you will need to do is develop a checklist of your daily and intraday procedures. You may respond by saying and even believing that what you do is so simple that no list is required; you have internalized everything you must do. I disagree. Even the simplest day trading method requires a checklist of procedures that should be written down either on paper or in a computer file and followed to the letter every time until the procedure has become automatic. Once that level of skill has been achieved and the list has become internalized, it will no longer be necessary to refer to the checklist unless the procedure changes or becomes more detailed, but that takes time.

The exact daily procedure you employ in your trading will depend on the methods, systems, and/or indicators you use. In some cases you will not be able to determine your trades until after markets open. In other cases you will have a very good idea of what trades you expect to make the next day. Regardless of when your initial screening or decisions are made, you must have a procedure in order to find your trades, or you will miss many opportunities. In previous chapters I have given you details regarding when trades are triggered. Those details will give you a very clear idea of what your daily procedure should be.

As an example, consider the gap trade described in Chapter 4. Inasmuch as a gap trade is not identifiable as such until a stock or commodity market has opened for the day, you cannot determine in advance which stocks or commodities will give you an entry setup. In order to do so you must wait until after the opening has occurred. If your trading software program has a filter or scan that will go through all markets looking for gap higher or lower openings, you can identify these candidates shortly after the markets open. If you are trading the gap method, that will be your daily procedure.

On the other hand, if you're trading the 30 MBO, you will not be able to determine a course of action until the first 30-minute price bar in the daytime session of E-Mini S&P has been completed. You will, however, be able to determine whether the trade is too risky by the end of the first price bar, possibly even on the opening of the first price bar. Therefore very early in the day session for E-Mini S&P, you will be able to determine whether there is a potential trade. If you have determined there is no possible trade for that day, you can move on to another trading method.

SPECIALIZATION

Another important aspect in the process of facilitating success as a day trader is specialization or, perhaps more accurately, focus. I have found that many traders attempt to trade as often as they can in as many markets as they can. Even with sophisticated computer programs, it is difficult for a trader to monitor more than a few markets and a few trades at any one time. It is far better to do a small number of things extremely well than a large number of things very poorly.

Whether you specialize in Forex, futures, or E-Mini S&P futures Treasury bonds, Treasury notes, currencies, or gold, the bottom line is that becoming proficient in one or several markets is important not only from the standpoint of consistency but also from the standpoint of avoiding confusion and having the time to correctly track and trade specific markets. Don't spread yourself too thin. You can do extremely well day trading only one market or one stock. The question naturally arises, what should you do if a number of opportunities present themselves at the same time? For example, after you do your daily computer scan for gap trade possibilities, you may find 15 or 20 or even more potential gap trades. Given that funds may be too limited to take all the trades, and it may be difficult if not impossible to enter all trades if they trigger, the decision should be made on the basis of which trade(s) trigger first and which trades have the least risk. Most traders make decisions based on which trades have the largest profit potential. As day traders—or, for that matter, traders of any type—our goal is first and foremost to manage risk. If we manage risk effectively and keep losing trades to a minimum while maximizing profits, we will eventually be successful. It's clear and obvious that if your risk is too high as a function of your account size, a series of losses will deplete your account to the point where no new trades are possible, which means you're out of the game.

PROFIT-MAXIMIZING STRATEGY

Without a profit-maximizing strategy, your experience will be exactly the same as that of the vast majority of day traders. You will have numerous small profits and a number of large losses. No matter how accurate your trading may be, the sum total of your profits ultimately will be lower than the sum total of the losses; losses without profit-maximizing strategies tend to be larger than profits. If you believe you are a good day trader because you have achieved 10, 15, or even 20 successive profitable day trades that dollar wise were relatively small, you may very well be wrong because your next trade may be a losing one that could be larger than all the profits of your previous 20 trades combined. This is a classic case of 15 small steps forward and a single large step back. If this is what is happening to you, clearly your profit-maximizing strategy is at fault, and you must change it.

Take a look at your account statements; they are there for a reason. Review them at the end of each month, or at the end of three months or six months or a year, if you prefer. Did you have any big winning trades? If you had no big winning trades, but you had many small winning trades and a few large losses, you are a typical day trader, and the probability is that you aren't making money. I am being brutally honest with you, and I suggest that you be brutally honest with yourself as well. Unless you do so, you will continue to labor under the false impression that you are a good trader or that you are making progress.

INCREASING POSITION SIZE

One of the concerns that traders often have is when to increase or decrease the size of their positions. Many traders find that as soon as they increase the size of their position—by which I mean the number of contracts or shares per trade—things seem to go astray and they begin to lose money. There are several ways to overcome this problem. Some trading software programs have a built-in feature that, based on a variety of performance metrics including the amount of money in your account, tells you how many contracts or shares should be traded on your next transaction. Many of these are based on the so-called Kelly formula. Another solution is to use a very simple rule of thumb: as soon as you have doubled your account size, you may increase the number of positions you trade by 25 percent.

Some people may think this approach is too conservative, but based on my experience it is realistic and very viable in making the trading size decision. Bear in mind that the system or method you are trading may also have certain position size requirements. As you know, I advocate trading in units of three, so I suggest when you double your account size you begin trading in units of four or, in stocks, 400 shares rather than 300, using the appropriate follow-through procedure on the last two units rather than on the last unit.

MICROMANAGING TRADES

Perhaps the most destructive and limiting behavior in which a day trader can engage is micromanaging positions. Once you have entered a position, whether that position is profitable or not at the time, there is a strong desire or tendency to begin looking at smaller and smaller time frames and more and more indicators to manage the position you have entered. You begin to look for reasons to get out of that trade in order to capture a profit. You become insecure and begin to wonder whether the small profit you are now enjoying will disappear and turn into a loss. In the back of your mind you hear the mantra you may have read in some trading book somewhere: "Do not let a profitable trade turn into a losing trade." The closer you look at prices, the more you will see.

In order to see the true picture, you need to step back and not micromanage the trade or look at informational inputs that are not part of your original process or trading decision. Remember, the trading method that got you into the trade should be the trading method that gets you out of the trade. The profit-maximizing and loss-minimizing strategy you have put into place are the only factors with which you should be concerned. If you truly want your day trading to be successful, you must not micromanage trades by looking at inputs that are not part of the original decision-making process. From small acorns large oak trees grow, but that doesn't happen immediately. They need time.

BEING VULNERABLE

Many traders tend to be insecure about their positions. If you are a position trader or investor, you're constantly looking over your shoulder, wondering if there's going to be bad news or good news that has an impact on your positions. You are exposed to a constant barrage of information in the form of international and national news, expert opinions on radio and television, Internet reports, and e-mails from anonymous sources or even from your brokerage firm or favorite advisory service. We are all vulnerable to errors and trading decisions that have nothing to do with the original decision to get into or out of the trade.

Some traders thrive on the news. As you read in Chapter 4, there are trading approaches based on news. Rather than reacting to the news to manage or mismanage a position I am already in, I use the news as a setup for a possible trade (i.e., gap trade as noted in Chapter 4). The difference between this method and being vulnerable to news is the same as the difference between being a professional and an amateur. The professional takes advantage of opportunities when they present themselves. The amateur reacts to situations rather than being proactive. Do your best to ignore stimuli that increase your vulnerability, and learn to use these situations as profit opportunities.

THE FALLACY OF THE DAILY GOAL

In Chapter 9 I discussed the fallacy of setting a daily profit goal for yourself. Many times what we hear about trading (and, in fact, in life itself) may sound good on the surface but, when examined closely, turns out to be bad thinking or an outright falsehood. The typical newcomer to day trading reasons that "If I can only make $500 a day, that would mean $2,500 a week times 50 weeks in the year, which adds up to a good amount of money. Therefore once I've reached my $500 a day target, I will stop my trading for the day." This is absolute nonsense and some of the worst thinking I've ever heard! Your goal as a day trader should be to make as much money as you possibly can every single day.

There is and should be no limit to how much you can achieve. To think that just because you have reached some arbitrary number and profit during a given day somehow limits what else you can make that day or sets you up for potential loss is magical and self-destructive thinking of the worst kind. Do not quit just because you believe you have reached the maximum of what you can make. If you have a method and a system, you must follow that method and system or you may find yourself leaving considerable money on the table.

CONCLUSION

With the advice in this chapter, you are now ready to continue your adventure with greater focus and renewed vigor. If your trading is already profitable, I hope some of my suggestions have been helpful. If your trading is not profitable yet, or if you're a newcomer and have not yet made your first trade, I believe this information will set you in the right direction. Indeed there are many things you can do. Your goal is to focus and do those things that are crystal clear to you, procedurally and operationally defined, and purely objective. In so doing you will emerge victorious in the long run if you have enough money in your account to see you through a series of losses in the short run.

CHAPTER 12

The Flat-Base Breakout for Day Trading

The majority of trading methods presented so far in this book have been as close to 100 percent objective as possible. I have indicated that the purpose of day trading position entry should be as mechanical as possible and as 100 percent rule based as possible, while exit strategies must be flexible and adjusted to market behavior. This approach to exit strategies is necessary because day traders are forced to be out of their trades by the end of the day, within the parameters of what we define as a day. However, I use and teach some day trading methods that I feel have potential as trading tools but are not as fully objective as I would like them to be. I do not recommend them for newcomers, but for the experienced day trader they offer potential provided they are applied consistently. One such method is the flat-base breakout (FB).

The FB was introduced by Joe Granville during his heyday as a prominent market technician. In the 1960s, when Joe did much of his work, the stock and commodity markets were not nearly as volatile as they are today. Prices were often prone to remain in sideways patterns or narrow trading ranges for extended periods of time. Joe observed that after a lengthy period of sideways movement, a breakout above a trading range often resulted in a large and sustained move to higher prices. I have studied the FB as a day trading entry signal and developed some rules and examples for its use.

Before examining these entry signals and rules, let's take a look at some FB patterns as they appear on a number of charts both within the day and other time frames. Figure 12.1 shows a monthly flat-base

F I G U R E 1 2 . 1

Flat-base pattern in monthly MTH

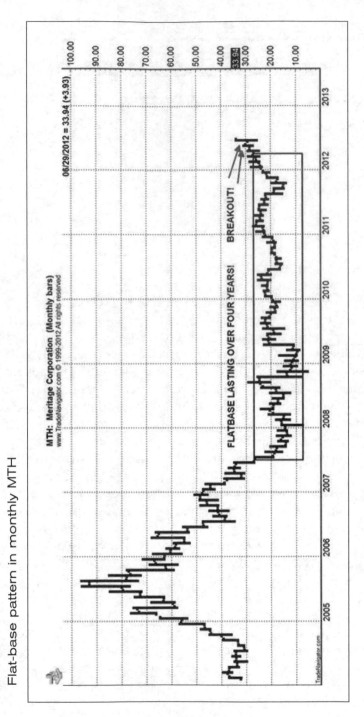

MTH: Meritage Corporation (Monthly bars)
www.TradeNavigator.com © 1999-2012 All rights reserved

06/29/2012 = 33.94 (+3.93)

BREAKOUT!

FLATBASE LASTING OVER FOUR YEARS!

TradeNavigator.com

pattern on MTH. I have marked the flat-base pattern, as well as the breakout above the flat base.

Observe three characteristics that are part and parcel of the FB pattern: First there must be an extended period of time during which prices tend to move in a sideways direction. By extended I mean at least 20 price bars within the time frame you are looking at. Second, there must be a relatively narrow trading range for that period of time. And third, there must be a breakout above the flat-base top, with a closing price above the highest price of the flat-base formation.

Figure 12.2 further illustrates the FB pattern on a 10-minute chart of the European currency futures. As you can see, I have marked the flat base, which is characterized by 20 price bars or more in a sideways pattern, which was then followed by two consecutive price bars closing above the highest price high during the FB pattern. Clearly the explosive move that followed was triggered by the FB pattern. I have noticed that the longer the FB takes to trigger, the more significant will be the subsequent move. This was suggested by Granville in his original work and confirmed in my conversations with him. It should also be noted that we are only discussing entry strategies at this point, without giving any attention as yet to exit strategies such as stop, trailing stop, or profit target. Two things are certain: as a day trader, you will need to find FB patterns within the day time frame, and you will need to exit your positions by the end of the trading day.

Now let's take a closer look at the short side of the FB pattern. In Granville's original work, he discussed the FB primarily as a buying opportunity. I have found that, although not as frequent, FB can precede a top and a subsequent market decline.

Figure 12.3, for example, shows a topping flat base followed by a trigger and a large subsequent down move in 10-minute Treasury bond futures. As you can readily observe, the setup and trigger procedures are similar to what has been described previously in Chapter 4. Also note that in this case, an exit at the end of the day would have not only been profitable but also close to the low of the day. Identifying an FB pattern is not completely objective, which is one of my biggest concerns about using this method. Traders should strive to develop as close to an operational procedure as possible without interpreting.

Now let's examine the flat-base pattern in E-Mini S&P futures using a five-minute chart. Many traders believe that trading more

FIGURE 12.2

Flat-base pattern in 10-minute euro currency futures

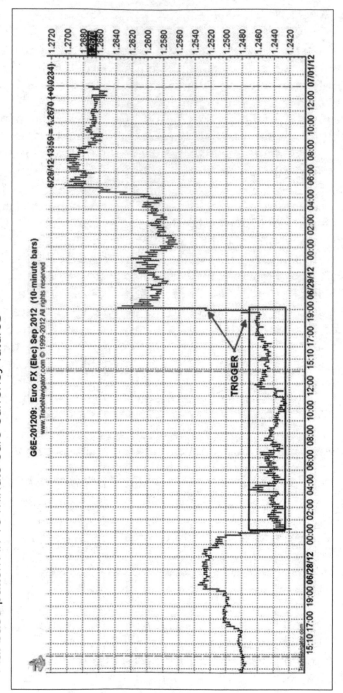

FIGURE 12.3

Flat-base pattern in 10-minute T-bond futures

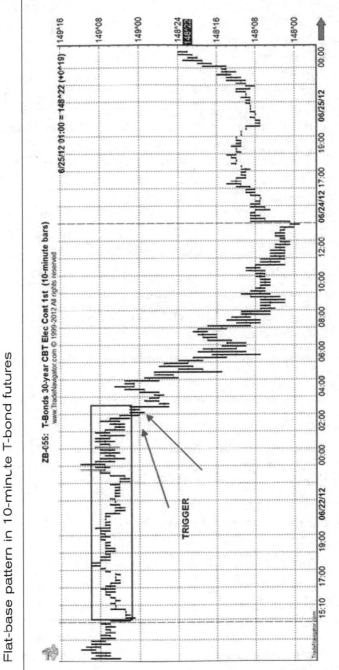

ZB-655: T-Bonds 30-year CBT Elec Cont 1st (10-minute bars)

frequently will result in more profits, which is not necessarily true. In fact in most cases I have observed just the opposite to be true. One way to reduce the number of trades is to use the FB, which takes time to develop. Figure 12.4 illustrates the flat-base pattern and breakout on a five-minute chart showing the FB, the trigger, and the subsequent move. Always remember that to use the FB as a day trading method, your position must be closed out prior to the end of the day.

The flat-base pattern is applicable to all time frames and all markets, whether stocks, stock indices, or Forex. Figure 12.5 illustrates the FB on a five-minute chart of Apple (AAPL). Once again I have identified the pattern, the breakout or trigger, and the follow through, showing exit at the end of the day.

Now let's review the FB and some rules of application. Here, in list form, is a summary of the procedure, as well as some suggestions based on my experience with the methodology:

- The FB is a sideways pattern that occurs over a period of 20 or more price bars in any time frame.

- A buy trigger occurs when there are two consecutive price bars closing above the high of the flat-base pattern.

- A long position is entered at market.

- A sell trigger occurs when there are two consecutive price bars closing below the low of the flat-base pattern.

- A short position is entered at market.

- A reasonable profit target for either a long or short position would be the range of the highest high to the lowest low during the period of the FB, which would also be a reasonable risk or stop loss.

- In order to maximize profit, a trailing stop should be implemented once the first profit target has been achieved. (See Figure 12.6.)

I have attempted to make this procedure as operational and mechanical as possible, but I completely understand it is subject to some degree of interpretation. That concerns me, but I believe that can be overcome by consistency and experience with the method. Given that the FB procedure is not nearly as mechanical as I would like it to be, practice and gain experience with it before implementation. Figure 12.6 illustrates the FB pattern with a first profit target and stop loss based on the information above.

FIGURE 12.4

Flat-base pattern in five-minute E-Mini S&P futures

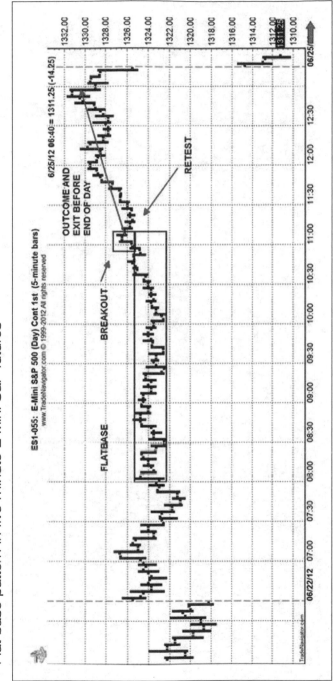

FIGURE 12.5

Flat-base pattern in five-minute AAPL

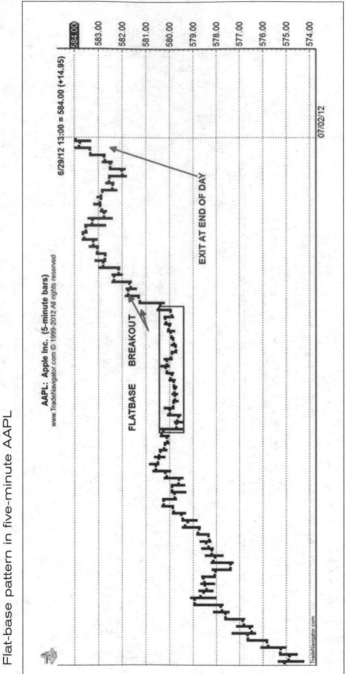

FIGURE 12.6

FB setup, trigger, and follow through to first target in four-minute crude oil futures

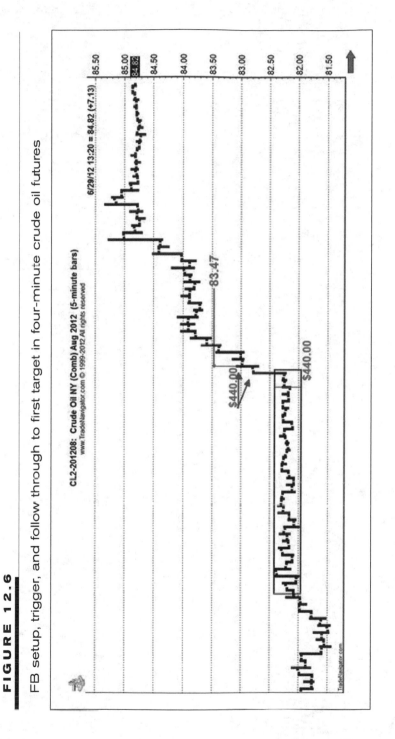

CL2-201208: Crude Oil NY (Comb) Aug 2012 (5-minute bars)

6/29/12 13:20 = 84.82 (+7.13)

83:47

$440.00

$440.00

CHAPTER 13

Momentum as a Day Trading Method: Two Applications

I have often been asked which timing indicators are my favorites. Given that there are so many, it would appear at first blush that the question might be difficult to answer. However, I do not find that to be the case at all. Most charting programs used by traders emphasize quantity over quality. A look at those programs verifies the fact that there are literally hundreds of choices available to traders. When it comes to their construction, the vast majority are based on price. Because they are based on price, they tend to trigger signals to buy or sell after a low or a high has been made. Because they lag price, they often "zag" when the market is "zigging" and vice versa, meaning that they tend to cause late entries and exits because they are not leading indicators. Consequently they are subject to frequent whipsaws. The chief complaint about lagging indicators such as traditional moving averages is that they tend to have very poor results in terms of accuracy.

TYPES OF TIMING TRIGGERS

All traders should be aware of the fact that there are three basic categories of timing triggers, which are determined by how soon or late they provide signals. Lagging indicators, as discussed above, are almost always late in entering a trade, whereas leading indicators are the exact opposite; their goal is to enter trades before markets change direction. Time-current indicators change direction with changes in market trends.

Here are a few examples of leading, lagging, and time-current indicators:

- Lagging indicators: moving averages, stochastic, RSI, and some chart-based indicators
- Leading indicators: price projections, cycles, seasonals, divergence indicators, and valid support- and resistance-based methods
- Time-current indicators: momentum, (moving average convergence divergence (MACD)), and indicators based on time of day or day of week

My assessment is certainly not written in stone nor is it complete. Although it is good to know the various categories of indicators, such knowledge is not necessary if you are aware of the assets and limitations of the indicator(s) you are using. The problem is one of lag time. There are a number of directions we can take in order to mitigate the lag-time issue, which is an especially significant one for the day trader who cannot afford to miss tops or bottoms, given that time runs out and trades must be exited by the end of the day. If the day trader is 25 percent late getting in after the start of a trend and 25 percent late getting out after the end of the trend, considerable opportunity has been left on the table, and when it comes to day trading, lost opportunities are lost money.

One direction that day traders can take is to use momentum-based timing triggers, which I believe not only are more accurate than moving average–based systems but also have less lag built into them and therefore result in fewer whipsaws.

Momentum (MOM), also referred to as rate of change (ROC), is a simple calculation or comparison of the price on any given day compared to the price X number of days ago. For MOM the calculation is a simple subtraction of the two values. For ROC the calculation is based on dividing the two numbers. Although the final values are different, the line plot on a graph is the same. Note that this is distinctly different than what is done in a moving average, in which all values over a certain period of time carry the same weight unless we are using a weighted or exponential moving average.

Momentum is a simple calculation that looks at only two values:

today and X days ago. For intraday charting we compare the current price bar with X price bars ago. As an example, if the closing price of the current bar is 50 and the closing price 10 bars ago also was 50, MOM equals zero. If the closing price 10 bars ago was 50 and the closing price of the current bar is 60, the MOM is +10. If the closing price 28 bars ago was 30 and the closing price of the current bar is 20, MOM is –10.

The relationship between momentum and price is a very simple one. Momentum in effect measures the willingness of buyers to keep buying at higher prices or the willingness of sellers to keep selling at lower prices. In order for prices to continue their upward movement, buyers must continue to buy at higher and higher prices, reflecting higher and higher momentum. The opposite holds true on the sell side. A market that is likely to keep trending higher will continue to show higher or sideways momentum as prices rise. A market that is likely to continue lower will keep showing lower and lower momentum or a sideways momentum at the very least.

The longer the length of the momentum, the less responsive the market will be to small changes in price. The shorter the length of the momentum, the more responsive the market will be to changes in price. As an illustration, see Figure 13.1, which shows several momentum lengths calculated on the same intraday chart. Note the similarities and differences between them.

As in the case of all timing indicators, it is important to find the optimum indicator length in order to get consistent results and to proceed operationally by specific rules. We do not want to change the momentum from one market to another in order to fit the indicator length; that would not give us results likely to go forward profitably.

There are normal and abnormal relationships between momentum and price. Figures 13.2 and 13.3 depict what I consider normal momentum relationships.

Between momentum and price is a very powerful indicator. Divergence, as defined for my purposes, is prices rising while momentum is falling or prices falling while momentum is rising. Each of these conditions tends to precede a change in direction. Additionally a change in momentum from a minus reading to a plus one tends to indicate a change in trend. Figures 13.4 and 13.5 illustrate these conditions on an intraday S&P futures chart.

FIGURE 13.1

Different momentum lengths and price

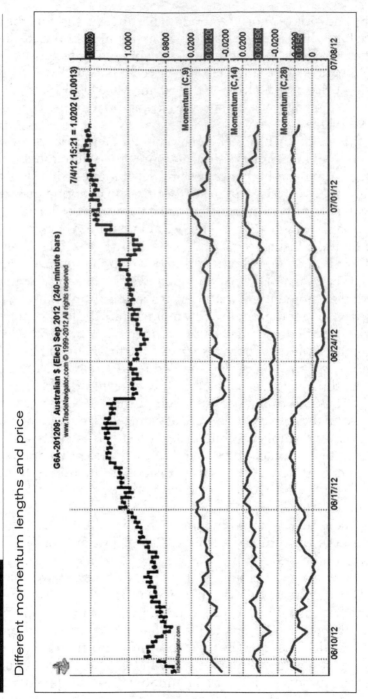

G6A-201209: Australian $ (Elec) Sep 2012 (240-minute bars)
www.TradeNavigator.com © 1999-2012 All rights reserved

7/4/12 15:21 = 1.0202 (-0.0013)

Momentum (C,9)

Momentum (C,14)

Momentum (C,26)

FIGURE 13.2

Normal bullish momentum configuration

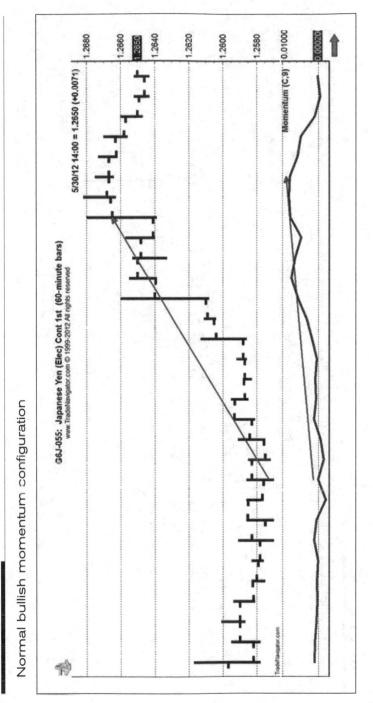

FIGURE 13.3

Normal bearish momentum configuration

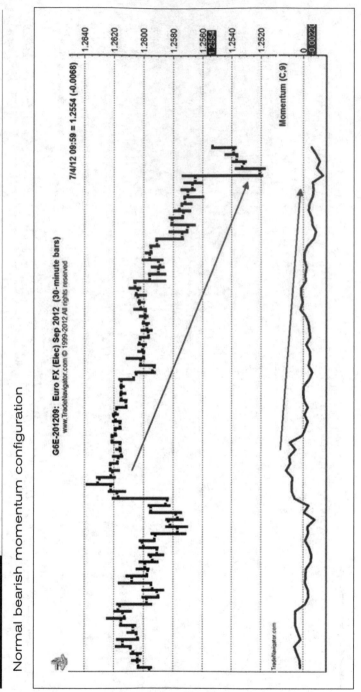

G6E-201209: Euro FX (Elec) Sep 2012 (30-minute bars)

7/4/12 09:59 = 1.2554 (-0.0068)

Momentum (C,9)

FIGURE 13.4

As prices rise momentum falls, a bearish leading indicator

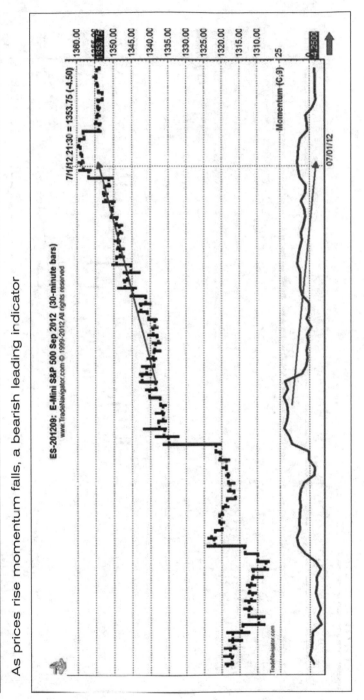

FIGURE 13.5

As prices fall momentum rises, a bullish leading indicator

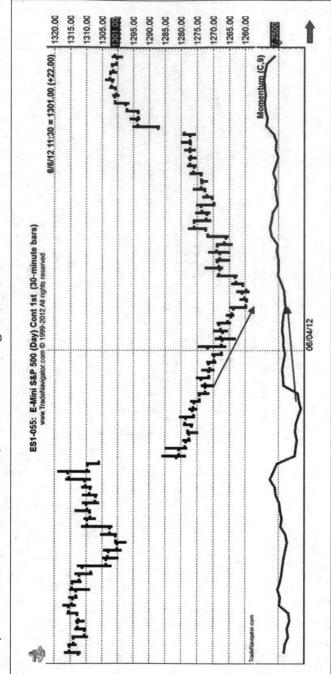

MOMENTUM CROSSING ABOVE OR BELOW ZERO

When momentum has been reading minus, as it usually does in a downtrending market, and changes direction, crossing back above zero, the odds are that a change in price trend from down to up has taken place. Conversely when momentum has been reading plus and crosses to minus, the odds are that a change in price trend from up to down has taken place. This relationship is not only easy to understand but can be used as a methodology for day trading. The application is simple, but it involves several decisions as well as a procedure to make it operational.

Given my earlier discussion about momentum and the direction of price, it is relatively easy to see that positive momentum will correlate with higher prices, while negative momentum will correlate closely with falling prices. Crossing from below the zero line to above it tends to trigger the start of new up moves, whereas crossing below zero from above it tends to trigger the start of a new downtrend. I've illustrated these signals in Figures 13.6 and 13.7.

Figure 13.6 shows the U.S. dollar 120-minute chart with momentum 28 crossovers above and below the zero line. I have marked several points of interest. The arrows show buy or sell signals when momentum crosses either above or below the zero line. As you can see, in each case the signal was accurate, resulting in a move as expected. However I have marked areas with boxes to illustrate some of the problems associated with this approach. Each of these areas indicates several buy and sell signals or whipsaws that would render the methodology considerably less accurate. This is one of the significant drawbacks of using momentum as a cross above or below zero to trigger signals.

Although not as serious, the whipsaw area shown in Figure 13.7 is still a significant limitation on the accuracy and implementation of zero-line momentum crossovers as a trading methodology. That's the bad news. The good news is that we can improve the situation by making some small but very effective changes in the momentum approach.

FIGURE 13.6

U.S. dollar 120-minute chart showing MOM 28 crossovers above and below zero

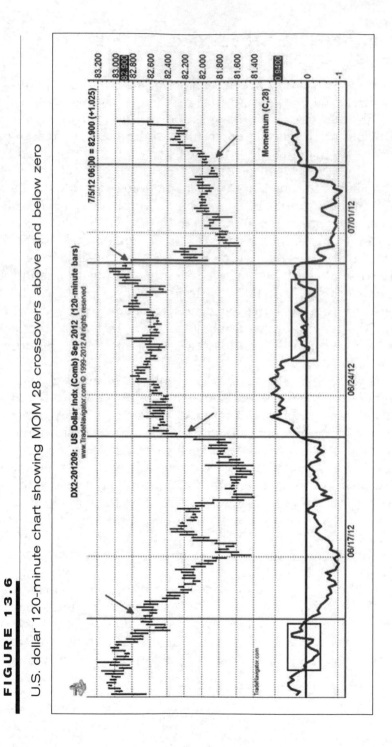

FIGURE 13.7

Crude oil 360-minute futures chart showing MOM 28 crossovers above and below zero

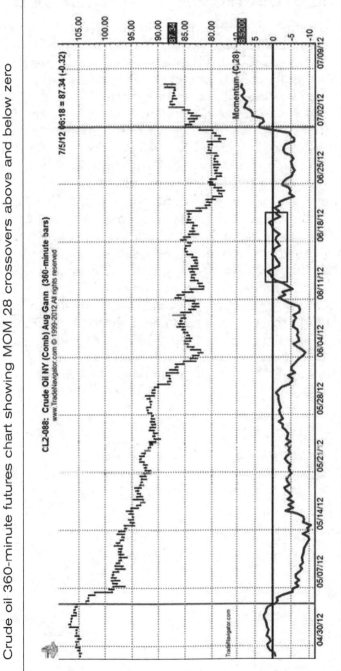

CL2-088: Crude Oil NY (Comb) Aug Gann (360-minute bars)
www.TradeNavigator.com © 1999-2012 All rights reserved

7/5/12 06:18 = 87.34 (-0.32)

Momentum (C,28)

MOMENTUM MOVING AVERAGE METHOD

The problems cited regarding momentum crossing above and below the zero line is not uncommon when it comes to oscillators using timing signals. This happens because they are too sensitive; desensitizing them has been one approach to solving the problem. Signals can be desensitized by either making the indicator length longer or by using a moving average of the indicator. By desensitizing an indicator, we also decrease its response time, which can also decrease its accuracy. I have developed a method for desensitizing the momentum indicator without seriously decreasing its accuracy: slow the indicator down with a moving average and then take a moving average of the moving average. The procedure, in other words, is to calculate momentum, take a moving average of momentum, and then take a moving average of the moving average of momentum. While this may sound like double talk, it significantly decreases erroneous signals and whipsaws and increases stability, provided you do it the right way.

Figure 13.8 illustrates this approach using a 30-minute E-mini S&P futures chart. I have annotated the chart to show buy and sell signals using this method. This approach is also shown in Figure 13.9. If you want to use this method of trading, then spend some time adding a follow-through aspect to further reduce whipsaw signals.

FIGURE 13.8

MOM 18 (not shown) with MA 9 and 7 of MOM as trigger signal

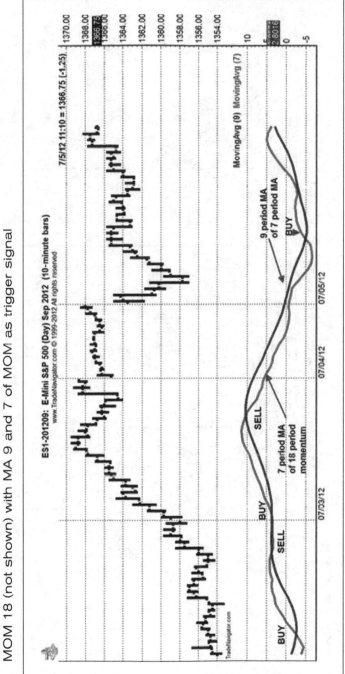

FIGURE 13.9

The dual MA of momentum method on USD/yen Forex six-hour chart

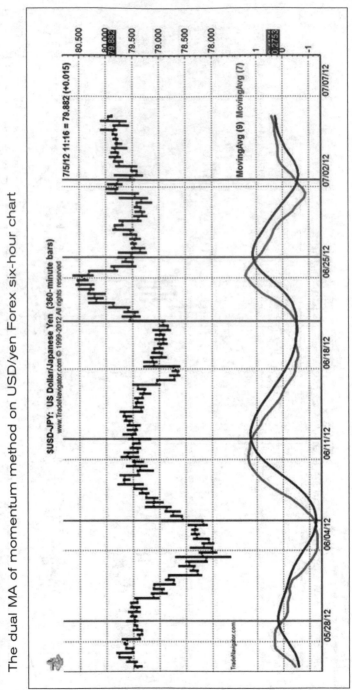

CHAPTER 14

Almost a Day Trade: Preholiday Seasonality

By definition a day trade is closed out at the end of the day; otherwise it's not really a day trade. The struggle—indeed the obstacle—constantly confronting the day trader is whether to hold a losing day trade beyond the end of the day in the hope that it will become profitable or, if profitable, to hold a day trade beyond the end of the day in the hope that it will become more so. Based on experience and statistical evidence, I believe a day trade held beyond the end of the day will not necessarily get better a predictably high percentage of the time. Therefore a day trade is a day trade is a day trade and must be closed out as a day trade if entered as a day trade. Regardless of statistics and experience, those nagging thoughts continue no matter how the day trade ends: Could the losing trade have turned into a winning one often enough to make riding the loss overnight a viable procedure? Could the winning day trade have turned into a bigger winner if kept beyond the end of the day? Can a winning day trade be the start of something much bigger, such as a position trade?

Other than the procedure of exiting a day trade on first profitable opening, which tends to force high accuracy, one of the best methods I know for holding a day trade overnight with high probability of the profitable exit the next day is a method based on preholiday seasonality. Originally discussed in his book, *The Behavior of Prices on Wall Street*, Art Merrill statistically demonstrated that the Dow Jones Industrial Average has shown a strong tendency to close higher on the day prior to major U.S. holidays. Although many traders are familiar with the work, not many are clear about how to use it.

In order to implement the Merrill preholiday seasonal effect correctly, you will be required to hold a position overnight. You must enter a position at the end of the day and exit at the end of the next day.

I have taken the research several steps further by applying my setup, trigger, and follow through methodology so that the procedure is operational and rule based. Obviously there are no guarantees that the method will continue to work, but as you can see from the statistical research I have performed, the probabilities are fairly significant. Judge for yourself after looking at what I have to offer.

First let's delineate the theory and then see how it plays out in practice. Merrill hypothesized and demonstrated to his satisfaction the following condition: the probability of the Dow Jones Industrial Average closing higher on the day prior to major U.S. holidays since the late 1800s has been statistically significant. Our goal is first and foremost to discover whether the statement is correct, then to see whether we can use that pattern profitably, and third to see whether we can develop a rule-based procedure regarding its application.

LOOKING AT THE FACTS

The following major U.S. holidays were examined for a period of about 60 years to determine the accuracy of Merrill's claim:

New Year's Day

Easter

Memorial Day

U.S. Independence Day

Labor Day

Thanksgiving

Christmas Day

Tables 14.1 to 14.8 display some results to examine:

TABLE 14.1

New Year's Day Seasonal Trade

Trades	62
Wins	34
Win %	55%

TABLE 14.2

Good Friday Seasonal Trade

Trades	62
Wins	45
Win %	73%

TABLE 14.3

USA Memorial Day Seasonal Trade

Trades	62
Wins	33
Win %	53%

TABLE 14.4

Independence Day Seasonal Trade

Trades	62
Wins	40
Win %	55%

TABLE 14.5

Veterans Day Seasonal Trade

Trades	62
Wins	32
Win %	52%

TABLE 14.6

Thanksgiving Day Seasonal Trade

Trades	62
Wins	45
Win %	73%

TABLE 14.7

Christmas Day Seasonal Trade

Trades	62
Wins	43
Win %	69%

TABLE 14.8

Labor Day Trade

Trades	62
Wins	44
Win %	71%

RULES OF APPLICATION

In order to operationalize the preholiday trade, I use the following rules:

- Enter on the close of trading on the day prior to the day prior to the legal holiday. If this sounds like double talk, I'll give you an example: Christmas occurs on December 25. If the market is open on December 24, enter on the close of trading December 23. Close out by the end of the day December 24.

- The trade is made either in a proxy for the Dow Jones Industrial Average—the diamonds (DIA)—or, if you prefer to trade futures, in the Dow Jones futures (YM), otherwise known as the five-dollar Dow.

- The trade can also be made in the S&P 100, the S&P 500 (SPY), or in an exchange-traded fund (ETF) related to the S&P or an ETF related to the Dow Jones Industrials (DIA).

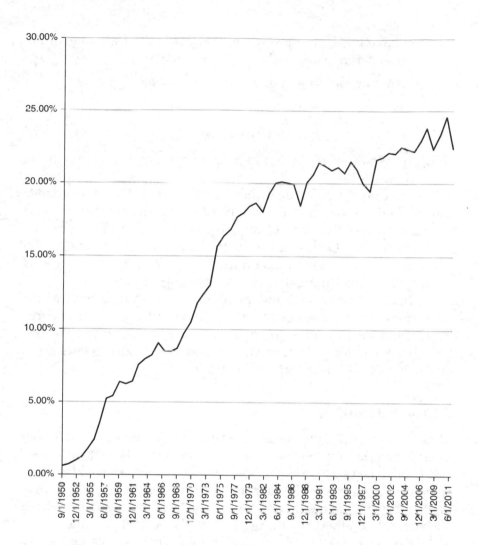

- The trade can also be made in the various stock or futures options most closely related to the Dow Jones Industrials.

- Entry is market on close on the entry date, as described earlier.

- Exit is at the market on close on the exit date, as described earlier.

- I have used a stop loss that is equal to the largest daily range of the 10 days preceding the trade.

- I have used a first profit target equal to 50 percent of the largest range of the 10 preceding days.

- I have used a full profit target equal to the full range of the largest range day of the 10 preceding days.
- I do not carry a winning trade beyond the exit date.

Examples

Here are two examples of the Independence Day preholiday trade for 2011 and 2012.

Based on the rules described earlier, the 2011 Independence Day trade entered at approximately 12,414 on the Dow and exited the next day on the close of approximately 12,588. These results are based on the Dow Jones Industrial cash index. Depending on whether the trade is executed on the DIA or YM, the dollar results would have been different but in any event profitable.

This chart shows the Independence Day trade in the YM for 2012. In this case the result yielded a $470 proximate profit according to the rules. Depending on how the trade was done, profit could have been smaller or larger as a function of the instruments used, but in any event it was a profitable trade.

CONCLUSION

My research verified the existence of preholiday seasonals in the Dow Jones Industrial Average, but as you can see from the statistics cited, you need to be selective. Some holidays researched showed less than 50 percent accuracy, while others have been very consistent and profitable. I believe there *is* preholiday seasonality, and that it is a viable and accurate methodology if used correctly. As stated at the beginning of the chapter, these are not day trades. There should be a study of the relationship between the opening price and the closing price on the day prior to the holiday; then the trade, provided it is accurate, could actually be implemented as a day trade.

FIGURE 14.1

The Independence Day 20⁻1 trade

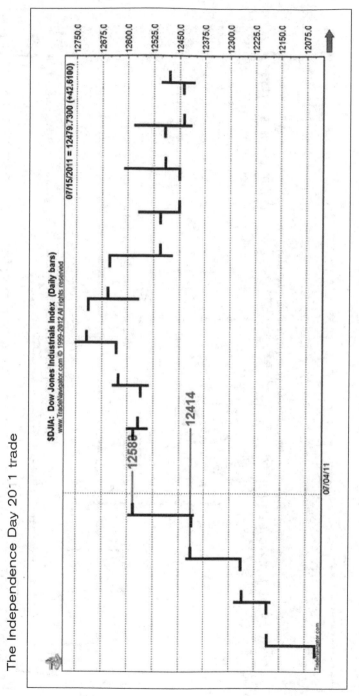

FIGURE 14.2

The Independence Day 2012 trade

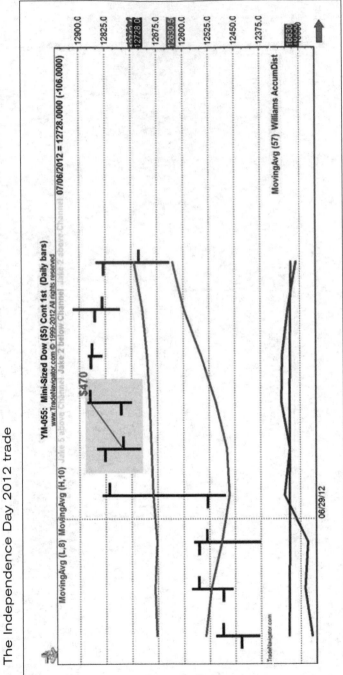

CHAPTER 15

Day Trading Do's and Don'ts

As I said in Chapter 9, there are many things a day trader can do incorrectly; there are relatively few things a day trader can do correctly. In this respect day trading is no different than life itself. We learn more from being rewarded for positive behaviors than we do from being punished for negative ones. This is one of the underlying principles of behavioral psychology, as so thoroughly expressed and espoused by B. F. Skinner, the so-called father of behavioral psychology. Profitable day trading is not entirely based on methodology. It is heavily dependent for its success upon proper procedures, flawless follow through, and a great deal of trader psychology.

Day traders tend to learn very little from their mistakes because there are literally hundreds of them that can be made, ranging from clerical errors to order entry errors to behavioral errors to position size errors. The best way to prevent errors is to recognize them before they are made. The best way to improve your day trading is to engage in positive behaviors that will be reinforced and therefore solidified through the reward of profits.

If you have read some of the many books that discuss the various rules for effective day trading, be prepared for something very different in this chapter. The traditional list of do's and don'ts is well known to most traders. Those who are new to the markets will either learn quickly or experience the don'ts directly, thereby learning from their profits and losses. While the traditional do's and don'ts are certainly important, I do not believe that they are fully understood by most day traders. In fact I find that most traders only give lip service to errors, which is why they continue to make the very same errors repeatedly. What follows is my list of do's and don'ts, along with detailed examples and explanations of each.

NEVER DAY TRADE ANY MARKET, STOCK, OR POSITION SIZE THAT SCARES YOU

As soon as you realize that you are trading a stock or commodity market that creates excessive fear of loss, consider this a warning that you are prone to making emotional decisions rather than objective ones. What could be the source of that fear? Previous bad experiences (for example, losses); extremely high volatility; very high price; the news backdrop for that particular market; too large a position size, or any number of other possible fear inducers. I have found that the best way to facilitate making objective decisions is to deal only with markets and position sizes that do not arouse fear. I differentiate here between fear and concern. Being concerned about losing money is normal. Being fearful about losing money prompts emotional decisions that may be bad for the health of your account.

It is very popular nowadays to day trade the currency futures markets, Forex, or S&P futures. Of the three, Forex is most adaptable to position sizes that will not prompt fear. You can commit to any position size you like when you trade Forex, provided you meet your broker's minimum account size.

Consider your fear and admit to it every time you trade. I reiterate that fear is often the leading emotional factor that inhibits success and contributes to losses. In the classic book *Reminiscences of the Stock Market Operator* by Edwin LeFevbre, he tells of the time Jesse Livermore was approached by another trader who claimed his position in a particular stock was so large that it caused him considerable anxiety, resulting in an inability to sleep. He asked Livermore what he could do. Livermore replied, "It's simple, sell down to the sleeping level." In other words, he told him to reduce his position size to the level at which the fear and anxiety disappeared.

DEFINE WHAT YOU MEAN BY A DAY TRADE AND STAY WITH THAT DEFINITION

This may seem like a ridiculous rule. After all, a day trade is a day trade, is it not? As I've discussed previously in this book, and as you most likely already know, trading hours vary significantly from one market to another. In stocks the trading day is clearly defined from the opening to the close of trading as a six-and-a-half-hour day, the exact times of which will vary based on your time zone. On the other hand, currency futures trade for 23 hours, while the Forex markets are essentially 24-hour markets. I do not consider the 23-hour session in currencies to be my trading day. My trading day in the currency futures is from the opening of the day session to the closing of the day session.

Depending on your quote vendor, there will be different symbols for the different sessions. I recommend using the day session symbols only. You cannot effectively day trade markets 23 hours a day. You need to get some sleep and rest. You must also day trade only during the active portion of the market session because that is when trading volume is at its peak, resulting in more accurate signals as well as more profitable entry and exit; the price spread between the bid and the offer in an active market is smaller, so better price executions are likely.

BE A SPECIALIST, NOT A GENERALIST

Most day trading methods require considerable attention during the course of the day. Positions must be monitored, targets in stocks must be changed, positions must be entered and exited, and you must do each flawlessly. Clerical errors often account for an unacceptable amount of losses. Even with the assistance of computer automation, it is not possible for most day traders to be in too many markets at the same time. Naturally if your day trading is fully automated and the computer is acting as a robot, entering and exiting trades for you, there may be virtually no limit to how many different markets you can trade at one time. Certainly that is possible, but for most traders it's not the recommended procedure, nor is it feasible, given their computer skills and equipment. My comments here are directed at the average day trader.

Your best results will be achieved through focus on several markets at the most. In fact, two or three markets are probably best. From my experience, you are far better off specializing in fewer markets and becoming experienced with them as opposed to trying everything. Much of what you do as a day trader will also depend on your methodology. For example, if you use the gap trade method, you can easily trade as many as 10 unrelated markets because all orders for exit and entry can be entered at the same time. I strongly urge the beginning day trader to focus on only a few trades at one time before expanding operations and running the risk of making costly clerical errors.

TRADE LESS AND MAKE MORE

The popular misconception that the more you trade the more you make is bound to get you into trouble. Remember that the faster you enter and exit trades, the less money you will likely make on each one. In order to compensate for the smaller move, you need to trade in the larger size. There is a clear and well-established relationship between how long you are in a trade and how much money you can make. The goal, of course, is to keep your winners as long as possible and to exit your losers quickly. There are some day traders who feel that the more trades they make each day as defined by entries and exits, the more money they will make. In my experience two to three day trades per day is more than enough to put you on the road to success provided you are using an effective profit-maximizing strategy.

REGULARLY REMOVE MONEY FROM YOUR ACCOUNT

As your account grows in size, give yourself a reward, taking advantage of the opportunity to take money from your account and either spend it or, even better, invest it in more secure areas. Let's face it: day trading is highly speculative; you can have large drawdowns, and you certainly don't want to give back all of what you have or more. With brokerage houses involved in fraud, scams, and various quasi-legal or illegal activities that have defrauded many investors of their funds, I believe it is prudent not to keep large sums of money with any one broker or in any one account. Furthermore, if you remove some of your profits regularly—I suggest monthly— you will have funds available in the event you need to recapitalize your account.

TRADE ENTRY RULES SHOULD BE FULLY OBJECTIVE, BUT TRADE EXIT RULES SHOULD BE FLEXIBLE

As I have indicated earlier in this book, exit strategies for day trading need to be more flexible than the ones for position trades because of the time restriction imposed on your trade. What you can do by the end of the day, when you need to be out of your position, is very much a function of what happens during the day. No two days will be exactly the same. I urge you to be flexible on your exit strategies, which should be adjusted to market behavior, keeping in mind the goal of either minimizing the loss and/or maximizing the profits when you exit your trades at the end of the day.

AVOID CHAT ROOMS

Day trading is a lonely as well as a loner's game. Unless you are especially strong psychologically, you will not find it possible to escape the influence of other traders' decisions and opinions on your own trading. I have been playing the day trading game for more than three decades and I can tell you based on personal experience, as well as what I have observed in thousands of other traders, that being influenced by outside opinion is detrimental to bottom-line results.

The growing popularity of social media websites, particularly chat rooms, may seem to offer excellent opportunities for traders and investors to share ideas and information. My experience and observations lead me to believe otherwise. In fact, I believe you should avoid participating in chat-room discussions unless you are a contrarian trader. Chat rooms are detrimental not only to results but also to your discipline as a trader. Before you participate in any such discussions, consider the fact that in most cases you are interacting with strangers who may have a vested interest in disseminating information that furthers their own self-interest and may be designed to tout the stocks or positions they are holding. My best advice is not to visit chat rooms at all.

DO YOUR OWN WORK

Too many aspiring and active day traders spend too much time and money searching for the Holy Grail. There are thousands of vendors out there in Internet land who will gladly sell you the perfect trading system or the most amazing timing trigger. I hope you have not fallen victim to such operators already.

ADDITIONAL WINNING AND LOSING BEHAVIORS

Below I offer you the following lists of winning and losing behaviors. Study and learn them; they will be very valuable to you. Let's start with the losers:

1. Small stop losses will protect you.
2. The more you trade, the more you make.
3. "I need to make $xxxxxx a month."
4. Options are the best way to trade.
5. My broker is there to help me.
6. A bigger and faster computer will help you make more money.
7. Day trading S&P is the best game in town.
8. The Forex market is the best market for profitable trading.
9. The 200-day moving average is a good way to trade.
10. Follow what the professional traders are doing, and you'll succeed.
11. The reversal and key reversal are profitable signals.
12. Spread trading is virtually risk free.

Additional potential blunders:

1. Lack of an objective profit-maximizing strategy
2. Lack of organization
3. Listening to the news
4. The "looks like" problem: opinions and interpretation
5. Lack of an objective trading method, system, or indicator
6. Too many indicators = too much "analysis"
7. Beginning with insufficient capital
8. Trading too many markets at once or the other side of the coin
9. Lack of diversification: the good and bad news of specializing
10. Failure to understand order types
11. Careless but costly errors
12. Impulsive behavior (trades not based on methods)
13. Excessive day trading
14. Low delta options: deep out of the money options
15. Stop losses that are too small to accommodate volatility
16. Trading markets that are too risky (e.g., new traders trading natural gas or full S&P, Forex)
17. Taking a quick profit in order to make your daily amount
18. Spreading to avoid taking a loss
19. Visiting a chat room and talking to losers or those who are there to tout their positions or spread disinformation or bad information
20. Lack of ability to take at least six losses in a row, otherwise known as insufficient trading capital and/or discipline.

And here is my list of winning behaviors:

1. Use the setup, trigger, follow through market structure, which uses a clear and concise profit-maximizing strategy.
2. Learn and use the "danger zone" concept.

3. Begin with sufficient capital (market conditions dependent).

4. Commit only 50 percent of your capital to positions, holding 50 percent in reserve.

5. Don't trade it if you can't test it: (a) what constitutes an adequate test? (b) do you need to back test with a computer program?

6. Use totally objective rules, or you will *fail; never* interpret anything; there is no "looks like."

7. Trade at least three unduplicated or uncorrelated markets.

8. Trade multiple positions if you can (units of three).

9. Avoid opinions; focus on facts.

10. Shut out the noise!

11. Use fewer, not more, indicators.

12. Don't trade anything that scares you.

13. Avoid common thinking; common thinking gets common results, and common results = losses.

14. Don't trade out of the money options unless you want to gamble; if you trade options as a buyer, use at or in the money (no more than one strike out of money at worst).

15. Get a trading partner if you can't pull the trigger.

16. Avoid chat rooms and blogs.

17. Mix time frames very carefully.

18. Analyze your results every month and make necessary changes.

19. Your stop loss must be a function of market volatility and/or a trading system, *not* a function of what you can afford to risk.

CHAPTER 16

High-Frequency Trading My Way

In previous chapters I have stressed the idea that day trading need not be something that makes you a slave to the computer. Whether you use the gap trade or the 30 MBO methods for your day trades, you will find that living and dying with every tick on the screen is not necessary for success as a day trader. Still there are those who cling to the idea that more is more when it comes to trading. They believe that the more you trade, the more you'll make. This will only be true if you trade large positions; smaller time frames yield smaller profits.

The price moves on a 30-minute moving average channel (MAC) chart, are considerably larger than the ones on a 10-minute MAC chart. Trading in the one-minute time frame is much faster, but unless position size is large, profits will be small on any given trade.

High-frequency trading, which now accounts for up to 70 percent of the trading volume at the New York Stock Exchange, has received considerable attention since the mid-to two thousands because it has allowed firms such as Goldman Sachs to reap billions of dollars in profits. While some believe that high-frequency trading games the system, others feel it provides much-needed liquidity and does not constitute an unfair advantage. Given that high-frequency traders buy and sell stocks within the time frame of fractions of seconds, usually 30 milliseconds, using information purchased from the exchanges, I believe that high-frequency trading depends on inside information and therefore constitutes an unfair advantage in a market that is supposedly based on a level playing field.

Using some of the methods discussed in this chapter, I feel the average trader can become a high-frequency trader without the need to buy inside information or sophisticated high-speed computers in order to process trades quickly. Although not nearly on the same level as high-frequency trading, my method is not so fast as to be outside the reach of the average trader.

MY HIGHER-FREQUENCY TRADING EXPERIMENT

Using my MAC method as described in Chapter 6, I was able to perform an interesting and profitable experiment that over the course of approximately eight weeks allowed me to begin my day trading higher-frequency adventure with a very small trading account and double it with very few losing trades. In discussing my methodology and sharing with you my purchase and sale statements from an actual account, I would like you to keep in mind the following three caveats:

1. What I'm about to show you is purely experimental and still in its early stages. I believe, however, that with some focus, practice, and consistency, the results will continue and any individual can replicate this performance.

2. I caution you not to attempt what I'm about to teach you unless you are able to be at the screen and computer constantly throughout the trading session and to do so every day without fail.

3. I will also hide behind the usual caveat that past performance is no guarantee of future results.

Having dispensed with the preliminary and obligatory public health warnings, here is the method I used, followed by some actual trades and account statements.

I used the MAC method according to the rules presented in Chapter 6. You'll recall that the MAC method is based on a 10-bar moving average of high prices and an eight-bar moving average of low prices combined with the Williams Accumulation Distribution and its moving average of 57. Two complete consecutive price bars above the top of the MAC constitute a buy trigger provided Williams AD is above its 57 moving average. Two complete consecutive price bars below the eight-period moving average of the low and Williams below constitute a sell trigger.

In the defined uptrend based on signals described above, this method attempts to buy at the eight-bar moving average of the low, with the profit target being the eight-bar moving average of the high. In a downtrend the 10-bar moving average of the high serves as resistance, and therefore it becomes a sell point.

I chose the futures market because there are no margin issues with regard to funds clearing for a day trade. As you should know, funds you use to enter a day trade in stocks are not immediately available for another day trade when you close that position. Those funds are not available to be used for three business days, which is not the case in futures. Therefore, beginning with a small account (about $4,700) for this higher-frequency trading experiment, I could trade as many times as I needed to during the day without having margin issues, as would be the case in stocks.

THE METHOD IN GREATER DETAIL

More specifically, I took the following steps:

1. I used the one-minute chart in order to generate trading opportunities during established trends.

2. As soon as a new trend was established based on the signals described above, I would either buy at support in a new uptrend or sell at resistance in the new downtrend.

3. I selected markets that were quick enough in their trading to allow for numerous opportunities but not so fast that I would find it impossible to get my orders entered and filled quickly enough.

4. I selected soybean oil futures, mini gold futures, and kept several others in abeyance, depending on how my experiment went.

Here is an example of the precise configuration I was look-ing for in order to make a trade. Figure 16.1 shows the one-minute chart of soybean oil futures on July 26, 2012.

This figure shows price in an up trend with Williams above its moving average. Subsequent to the buy trigger, there were numer-ous declines to the bottom of the MAC, which were then followed by rallies back to the top of the MAC, each of which constituted an opportunity to do a high-frequency trade, buying at the MAC bot-tom and getting out at the top.

These opportunities translated to very short-term high-frequency swing trades shown in Figure 16.2. The illustration in Figure 16.1 is for the September futures contract. I used the August futures contract in my work and in the trades shown in Figure 16.2 due to higher volume and liquidity.

Let's examine another example of what I was looking for. Figure 16.3 shows a similar configuration in gold futures, offer-ing numerous opportunities for high-frequency trades swinging back and forth within the channel, buying at support and exiting at resistance.

Here is a list of some trades that were made consistent with swing trade channel (Figure 16.3) on August 1, 2012 (Figure 16.4).

During the period of my high-frequency trading experiment, I was able to achieve extremely positive results. Figures 16.5 and 16.6 show the starting balance and current balance as of the state-ment date indicated. I would be very happy if I could say that this was achieved using strictly mechanical rules, but this was not the case. I did use one additional tool in my work, the depth of market assessment, which allowed me to view important infor-mation on resting orders above and below the current price. The depth of market tool I used was CQG DOMTRADER™. With it I was able to determine if there was significant price competition at specific price levels where I wanted to buy or sell. If, for example, I wanted to buy at a particular price but observed there were several hundred orders to buy at that price, I deferred my decision and attempted to buy one price tick higher or even two ticks higher, provided there were significantly fewer orders at those prices. I combined the science of the indicators and the signals with some experience in order to execute the trades.

FIGURE 16.1

One-minute MAC with Williams AD and its MA soybean oil futures, July 26, 2012

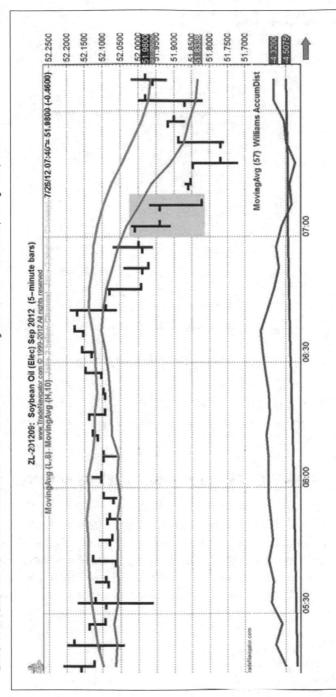

FIGURE 16.2

High-frequency trades in August soybean oil on July 26, 2012, using my high-frequency trading approach

```
- - - -BUY SELL - - - -  P U R C H A S E  &  S A L E - - - - - - - - - - - -
   7/26    1            AUG12 CBT SOYOIL    S         51.66
   7/26    1            AUG12 CBT SOYOIL    S         51.69
   7/26    1            AUG12 CBT SOYOIL    S         51.83
   7/26    1            AUG12 CBT SOYOIL    S         51.84
   7/26    1            AUG12 CBT SOYOIL    S         51.85
   7/26    2            AUG12 CBT SOYOIL    S         51.86
   7/26    4            AUG12 CBT SOYOIL    S         51.87
   7/26    1            AUG12 CBT SOYOIL    S         51.88
   7/26    2            AUG12 CBT SOYOIL    S         51.89
   7/26         2       AUG12 CBT SOYOIL    S         51.82
   7/26         1       AUG12 CBT SOYOIL    S         51.89
   7/26         3       AUG12 CBT SOYOIL    S         51.91
   7/26         4       AUG12 CBT SOYOIL    S         51.92
   7/26         1       AUG12 CBT SOYOIL    S         51.93
   7/26         1       AUG12 CBT SOYOIL    S         51.94
   7/26         1       AUG12 CBT SOYOIL    S         52.02
   7/26         1       AUG12 CBT SOYOIL    S         52.08
         14*   14*                              P & S         708.00 *
         TOTAL COMM/FEE                         NET P&L       708.00 *
- - - - - - - - - - - - - - - - - - - - - - - - - - - - - - - - - - - - - -
 CURR BAL US DOLLARS FUNDS-Segregated Accounts US            7,510.27
```

Another Example

Here is another example of my methodology as applied to mini gold futures on July 20, 2012. Figure 16.7 shows the results, and Figure 16.8 shows a portion of the one-minute swing trade chart for that day.

SUGGESTIONS FOR IMPLEMENTATION

While I'm a strong believer in the objective and mechanical approach to trading, day trading combines mechanical entry and less mechanical exit methods. In the case of high-frequency trading, both entry and exit methods can combine mechanical as well as judgment-based decisions that although not fully objective can be learned by trial and error. Television commercials featuring daredevil stunt drivers are quick to point out that the commercial was filmed on a closed course and that viewers are advised "not to try this at home."

If you are an ambitious and motivated day trader seeking to improve your results, you do want to try this at home, but

FIGURE 16.3

A bullish configuration and swing trade channel to buy the MAC low and exit at the MAC high after a moving average channel by setup and trigger

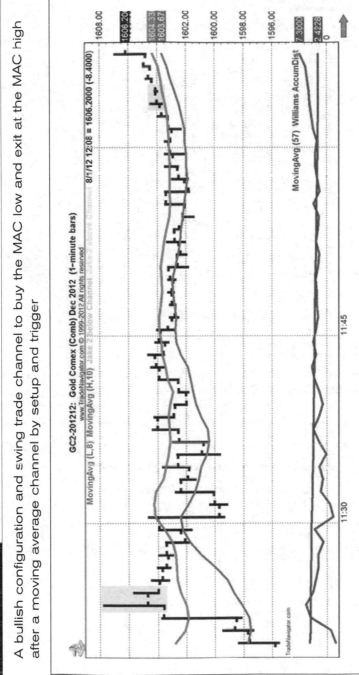

GC2-201212: Gold Comex (Comb) Dec 2012 (1-minute bars)
www.TradeNavigator.com © 1999-2012 All rights reserved   8/1/12 12:08 = 1606.2000 (-8.4000)

MovingAvg (L,8) MovingAvg (H,10) Jake 2 below Channel Jake 2 above Channel

MovingAvg (57) Williams AccumDist

TradeNavigator.com

FIGURE 16.4

High-frequency gold trades, August 1, 2012

```
- - - -BUY SELL - - - -  P U R C H A S E  &  S A L E - - - - - - - - - - - -
  8/01    1           AUG12 CBT SOYOIL   S        52.22
  8/01          1     AUG12 CBT SOYOIL   S        52.24
         1*     1*                                P & S              12.00 *
  8/01    1           DEC12 CBT SOYOIL   S        52.79
  8/01          1     DEC12 CBT SOYOIL   S        52.92
         1*     1*                                P & S              78.00 *
  8/01    1           DEC12 NYSE MGOLD   G      1597.30
  8/01    1           DEC12 NYSE MGOLD   G      1599.80
  8/01    1           DEC12 NYSE MGOLD   G      1600.70
  8/01    1           DEC12 NYSE MGOLD   G      1600.90
  8/01    1           DEC12 NYSE MGOLD   G      1601.00
  8/01    1           DEC12 NYSE MGOLD   G      1601.10
  8/01    1           DEC12 NYSE MGOLD   G      1601.20
  8/01    1           DEC12 NYSE MGOLD   G      1601.60
  8/01    1           DEC12 NYSE MGOLD   G      1603.10
  8/01          2     DEC12 NYSE MGOLD   G      1601.80
  8/01          5     DEC12 NYSE MGOLD   G      1602.00
  8/01          1     DEC12 NYSE MGOLD   G      1602.10
  8/01          1     DEC12 NYSE MGOLD   G      1602.20
         9*     9*                                P & S             371.84 *
              TOTAL COMM/FEE                      NET P&L           461.84 *
- - - - - - - - - - - - - - - - - - - - - - - - - - - - - - - - - - - - - -
  CURR BAL US DOLLARS FUNDS-Segregated Accounts US                7,982.94
```

FIGURE 16.5

Starting balance in the high-frequency trading experiment account, July 10, 2012: $4780.44

```
=================================================================================
     BERNSTEIN              501C              7/11/12
  7/10/12 US DOLLARS FUNDS-Segregated Accounts US                  4,780.44
- - - -BUY SELL - - - - - - C O N F I R M A T I O N - - - - - - - - - - - - -
WE HAVE MADE THIS DAY THE FOLLOWING TRADES FOR YOUR ACCOUNT AND RISK.
         1          AUG12 NYSE MGOLD   G      1570.00
              1     AUG12 NYSE MGOLD   G      1571.40
              1     AUG12 NYSE MGOLD   G      1573.50
        1*    2*  COMM/FEE               7.76-
              TOTAL COMM                 1.40-*
              NFA                         .06-*
              TRAN FEE                   5.55-*
              ROUTINGFEE                  .75-*
              TOTAL COMM/FEE             7.76-                          *
- - - -BUY SELL - - - -  P U R C H A S E  &  S A L E - - - - - - - - - - - -
  7/10    1          AUG12 NYSE MGOLD   G      1569.90
  7/11    1          AUG12 NYSE MGOLD   G      1570.00
  7/11         1     AUG12 NYSE MGOLD   G      1571.40
  7/11         1     AUG12 NYSE MGOLD   G      1573.50
        2*    2*                                 P & S             166.00 *
              TOTAL COMM/FEE                     NET P&L           166.00 *
- - - - - - - - - - - - - - - - - - - - - - - - - - - - - - - - - - - - - -
  CURR BAL US DOLLARS FUNDS-Segregated Accounts US                4,938.68
```

FIGURE 16.6

High-frequency trading account balance, August 24, 2012:
$10,432.96

```
- - - -BUY SELL - - - -  P U R C H A S E   &   S A L E - - - - - - - - - - - - -
  8/24    1              DEC12 CBT SOYOIL    S        56.66
  8/24    1              DEC12 CBT SOYOIL    S        56.67
  8/24    1              DEC12 CBT SOYOIL    S        56.79
  8/24    1              DEC12 CBT SOYOIL    S        56.84
  8/24    2              DEC12 CBT SOYOIL    S        56.85
  8/24           1       DEC12 CBT SOYOIL    S        56.72
  8/24           1       DEC12 CBT SOYOIL    S        56.75
  8/24           2       DEC12 CBT SOYOIL    S        56.86
  8/24           1       DEC12 CBT SOYOIL    S        56.87
  8/24           1       DEC12 CBT SOYOIL    S        56.88
           6*   6*                          P & S                168.00 *
  8/24    1              DEC12 NYSE MGOLD    G      1667.30
  8/24    1              DEC12 NYSE MGOLD    G      1669.20
  8/24    1              DEC12 NYSE MGOLD    G      1669.50
  8/24           1       DEC12 NYSE MGOLD    G      1667.80
  8/24           1       DEC12 NYSE MGOLD    G      1670.00
  8/24           1       DEC12 NYSE MGOLD    G      1670.20
           3*   3*                          P & S                 66.40 *
           TOTAL COMM/FEE                   NET P&L              234.40 *
- - - - - - - - - - - - - - - - - - - - - - - - - - - - - - - - - - - - - - - -
CURR BAL US DOLLARS FUNDS-Segregated Accounts US                10,432.96
```

with all the appropriate precautions. Practice this with simulated
trading and develop your style before you risk a single penny on
any of these methods. I believe this method can be learned, but
more so than any other method I know, experience is absolutely
essential.

I do not believe that two day traders trading the same approach
will always reach the same conclusion. I do believe that if the methodology has been developed within their trading style and their
understanding of the general rules is clear, they can achieve generally similar outcomes.

Finally I realize that the profit achieved in this high-frequency
trading account is small dollar wise but large in terms of percentage
gain. I firmly believe that if you're going to test this or any other
method in real time you do so with money that is pure risk capital
and moreover innocuous in terms of the emotional consequences
that losses may cause. My final words to you on this or any of the
other methods I have shown you is to practice as much as possible
and only with funds you can truly afford to lose.

FIGURE 16.7

Gold futures high-frequency trading results, July 20, 2012

```
- - - -BUY SELL - - - -   P U R C H A S E   &   S A L E - - - - - - - - - - - -
  7/20    1              AUG12 NYSE MGOLD      G      1575.20
  7/20    1              AUG12 NYSE MGOLD      G      1575.30
  7/20    1              AUG12 NYSE MGOLD      G      1575.70
  7/20    2              AUG12 NYSE MGOLD      G      1575.80
  7/20    1              AUG12 NYSE MGOLD      G      1575.90
  7/20    2              AUG12 NYSE MGOLD      G      1576.80
  7/20    1              AUG12 NYSE MGOLD      G      1577.60
  7/20    1              AUG12 NYSE MGOLD      G      1580.60
  7/20         1         AUG12 NYSE MGOLD      G      1576.00
  7/20         1         AUG12 NYSE MGOLD      G      1576.20
  7/20         1         AUG12 NYSE MGOLD      G      1576.50
  7/20         1         AUG12 NYSE MGOLD      G      1576.70
  7/20         2         AUG12 NYSE MGOLD      G      1576.80
  7/20         1         AUG12 NYSE MGOLD      G      1577.50
  7/20         1         AUG12 NYSE MGOLD      G      1577.60
  7/20         1         AUG12 NYSE MGOLD      G      1578.50
  7/20         1         AUG12 NYSE MGOLD      G      1581.90
         10*  10*                                P & S        298.80 *
              TOTAL COMM/FEE                    NET P&L       298.80 *
- - - - - - - - - - - - - - - - - - - - - - - - - - - - - - - - - - - - - - - - -
CURR BAL US DOLLARS FUNDS-Segregated Accounts US              6,341.07
```

FIGURE 16.8

Gold futures portion of one-minute chart, July 20, 2012

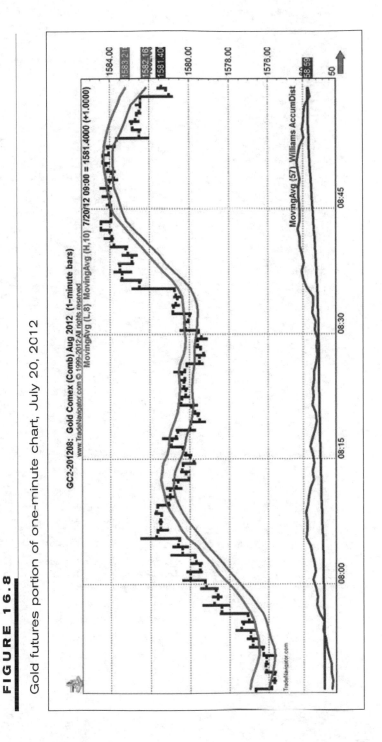

GC2-201208: Gold Comex (Comb) Aug 2012 (1-minute bars)
www.TradeNavigator.com © 1999-2012 All rights reserved
MovingAvg (H,10) 7/20/12 09:00 = 1581.4000 (+1.0000)
MovingAvg (L,8)

MovingAvg (57) Williams AccumDist

TradeNavigator.com

CHAPTER 17

Critical Elements for Success as a Day Trader

My many years as a trader in stocks and futures have been not only incredibly enjoyable but also a constant learning experience. I have benefited from my own mistakes and from the mistakes of others. Having personally mentored hundreds of traders over the years, and having coached traders on a one-on-one basis, I have been blessed with countless opportunities to observe not only the repetitive errors that traders make but also the relatively few things traders do that lead to profits.

The sad truth is that most day traders lose money. They do not lose because their techniques are useless, but their losses can be attributable to various and sundry other reasons not directly related to methodology. I maintain that the primary reason for traders' losses is psychological or behavioral. My observation of my own trading, as well as the trading of hundreds of others, leads to the inescapable conclusion that several behavioral factors either limit success or inhibit it entirely, while others enhance success.

Here is a brief list of those limiting factors, not necessarily in order of importance:

1. Insufficient starting capital

2. Failure to do trading homework

3. Errors in order placement

4. Mathematical errors

5. Errors caused by failing to follow a trading system

6. Responding to rumors

7. Overextending margin

8. Premature entry or exit

9. Failure to maintain a trading plan

10. Disorganization

11. Lack of attention to detail

12. Adding to losing positions

13. Placing a spread in order to avoid taking a loss

14. Entering a trade with one method and exiting it with another

These are, of course, relatively broad categories of error within which are literally dozens of others. As I have already said, there are hundreds of things a trader can do wrong but very few things he can do right. As used in this context the term *right* means profitable.

I believe that we can unlearn many if not most losing habits and replace them with winning ones, but in order to do so we need to know what the winning habits are. We need to know them exactly—step by step or word for word or behavior for behavior. We need to know the broad categories of losing habits as well as the behaviors that fall within those broad categories. While it may be true that some great traders are born that way, I believe great traders can be created through education. Beyond methodology, behavior is the strongest as well as the weakest link in the trading chain.

A FEW WORDS ABOUT LEARNING

In my "former life," I worked in the mental health field. My clients included institutionalized psychotic individuals as well as children with severe developmental disabilities such as autism in its various forms and numerous self-abusive behaviors. Some people have joked that I do the same kind of work now but I get paid better. All levity aside, I do believe there are parallels between some of the behaviors that afflict the seriously ill and the ones in which traders engage. I believe it's mostly about learning.

While some seriously dysfunctional human behaviors are the result of congenital or genetic defects, such issues are generally not part of the underlying etiology of trading behavior dysfunctions. I believe it is much easier to solve dysfunctional trading behavior than the dysfunctional psychological behavior in clinical patients. I have been able to use my observations of the chronically psychologically ill in the remediation of trading behavior dysfunctions. Putting on my behavioral learning theorist hat for a while, I would like to share with you what I have learned about what can and should be learned, as well as what should be unlearned in regard to trading.

There are several ways in which we can learn things. Our educational system all too often focuses on punishing the negative as opposed to rewarding the positive. Behavioral psychologists agree that positive reinforcement of desired behaviors is much more effective than punishing negative behaviors. And the combined effect of reinforcing or rewarding the positive while at the same time punishing the negative is more powerful and lasting than either alternative by itself.

If you think about losing money as a punishment for bad behavior, you may also conclude that if you get punished for specific bad behavior you will not repeat it. As a concrete example, consider the following: a trader reacts to a recommendation on CNBC to buy a particular stock. She is aware of the fact that to act on that recommendation without first checking her trading indicators is contrary to the rules. Overcome by greed, however, the trader buys the recommended stock only to see it move against her. Within minutes a $300 loss has occurred.

At this juncture the trader can commit either of several additional errors:

1. Adding to the losing position

2. Holding the stock overnight rather than as a day trade

3. Exiting the stock prior to the initial stop loss

4. Buying an option against the position to avoid the loss becoming worse

5. Exploring other avenues to avoid taking the loss

Assume, however, that the one error did not lead to a series of others, as is usually the case. Assume the trader admitted to her error and exited the stock immediately, taking the loss while it was still relatively small. One would assume that the punishment—losing money—would be a sufficient learning experience to result in the trader never engaging in that sort of behavior again. Sadly, this is rarely the case. Why? The trader has experienced previous bad learning by engaging in this behavior and has been rewarded for it by making money. Sometimes she loses, sometimes she wins. She has no idea when she will win or when she will lose. This type of faulty learning is the most difficult to undo. It is behavior that has been maintained on what is termed a partial random reinforcement schedule.

Thousands if not hundreds of thousands of traders engage in this sort of behavior virtually every minute of every day. Perhaps you have done so yourself. There are several potential cures for this behavior. Let's look at some of them:

1. You can entirely avoid this kind of behavior by not watching business television shows that have in the past led you to engage in it.

2. If this behavior was prompted or motivated by visiting Internet chat rooms where traders engage in meaningless, self-serving, cathartic ramblings, you can avoid visiting chat rooms.

3. If you must do both of the above, at the very minimum consider the recommendation or tip to be a "setup" or pattern that must be triggered and followed through, as explained in my STF trading model

Unless this type of behavior is extinguished entirely, this most common of losing behaviors will continue, and it will not only inhibit performance but also frequently undermine results and erode self-confidence, which will further erode self-discipline and results.

Let's take a look at another example of how being punished for losing behavior by losing money fails to teach you anything. Consider the trader who enters an order incorrectly. Within minutes after the trade has been executed, it begins to move against him. While recognizing that the trade is going wrong, he fails to understand why it is happening. After all, the system says the trade should work. The stop loss is in place and the trade gets stopped out at a loss. The trader does not understand what happened. Why was there a loss? He knows there are two types of broad categories that cause losses. The first one is the smart loss. Money was lost because the trading system failed on that particular occasion. Knowing that trading systems are far from perfect, the trader can accept that the system will not work 30 percent of the time or even more.

The second right category of loss-producing factors is what I have referred to as the stupid loss. It occurs as a function of trader behavior rather than system behavior. In this case the system lost money, but the trader lost even more money than the system was supposed to lose. By failing to keep a record of his behavior, the trader unfortunately cannot determine where in the process he went wrong. Unless he is able to recreate the exact sequence of steps that caused the loss, the trader will fail to learn anything from his punishment.

Perhaps the single best way to avoid most of the problems that result in trading losses is through clarity and organization of trading decisions from before the start of a trade until after the end of the trade. This speaks strongly to the case that favors organization and procedural steps when it comes to trading. This is even more important to the day trader than it is to the investor or the short-term or position trader. Why is this so? The answer is, of course, that day trading is a very intense form of trading with decisions frequently having to be made on a moment-to-moment basis. Although I do not consider myself to be a tame day trader, only entering into one or two day trades per day, I'm also not a particularly manic one, who engages in hundreds of day trades per day.

Figures 17.1 through 17.5 show a few of my futures day trades in one of my smaller accounts to illustrate the frequency with which trades can occur even in a small account.

Even a small number of day trades such as those illustrated in Figures 17.1 through 17.5 in a relatively small account require the utmost organization and planning. When trades are entered and exited within a matter of minutes or even seconds, it is critically important to be completely organized, keeping track of your positions in order to avoid making costly errors. This can only

FIGURE 17.1

Some day trades in futures on June 15

Day Trades 6/15
296VM 982 6/15/10 CQG 15 June
----BUY SELL------C O N F I R M A T I O N---
6/15 WE HAVE MADE THIS DAY THE FOLLOWING
6/15 1 SEP10 CBT T-BOND S 122.21
6/15 1 SEP10 CBT T-BOND S 122.22
6/15 1 SEP10 CBT T-BOND S 122.23
6/15 3 SEP10 CBT T-BOND S 122.25
6/15 2 SEP10 CBT T-BOND S 122.27
6/15 1 SEP10 CBT T-BOND S 123.00
6/15 1 SEP10 CBT T-BOND S 122.22
6/15 2 SEP10 CBT T-BOND S 122.24
6/15 2 SEP10 CBT T-BOND S 122.26
6/15 1 SEP10 CBT T-BOND S 122.27
6/15 2 SEP10 CBT T-BOND S 122.28
6/15 1 SEP10 CBT T-BOND S 123.01
6/15 9* 9* COMM/FEE 72.18-
6/15 1 SEP10 IMM A-DLLR G .84800
6/15 1 SEP10 IMM A-DLLR G .84830
6/15 1 SEP10 IMM A-DLLR G .84890
6/15 1 SEP10 IMM A-DLLR G .84970
6/15 1 SEP10 IMM A-DLLR G .85100
6/15 1 SEP10 IMM A-DLLR G .85160
6/15 1 SEP10 IMM A-DLLR G .84840
6/15 1 SEP10 IMM A-DLLR G .84930
6/15 1 SEP10 IMM A-DLLR G .84950
6/15 1 SEP10 IMM A-DLLR G .85020
6/15 1 SEP10 IMM A-DLLR G .85140
1 SEP10 IMM A-DLLR G .85240
6* 6* COMM/FEE 48.12-
TOTAL COMM 120.00-*
NFA .30-*
TOTAL COMM/FEE 120.30- *
----BUY SELL----P U R C H A S E & S A L E---
6/15 1 SEP10 CBT T-BOND S 122.21
6/15 1 SEP10 CBT T-BOND S 122.22
6/15 1 SEP10 CBT T-BOND S 122.23
6/15 3 SEP10 CBT T-BOND S 122.25
6/15 2 SEP10 CBT T-BOND S 122.27
6/15 1 SEP10 CBT T-BOND S 123.00
6/15 1 SEP10 CBT T-BOND S 122.22
6/15 2 SEP10 CBT T-BOND S 122.24
6/15 2 SEP10 CBT T-BOND S 122.26

be achieved by having a specific plan, as well as a record-keeping system that allows you to keep track of your trades. And this end can be relatively easily achieved through the online account tracking your broker most likely has for your account. If you do have such a feature, learn how to use it and understand exactly how your positions are reported to you; there are differences from one

FIGURE 17.2

Some day trades in futures on June 15 (continued) and June 16

```
6/15 1 SEP10 IMM A-DLLR G .84800
6/15 1 SEP10 IMM A-DLLR G .84830
6/15 1 SEP10 IMM A-DLLR G .84890
6/15 1 SEP10 IMM A-DLLR G .84970
6/15 1 SEP10 IMM A-DLLR G .85100
6/15 1 SEP10 IMM A-DLLR G .85160
6/15 1 SEP10 IMM A-DLLR G .84840
6/15 1 SEP10 IMM A-DLLR G .84930
6/15 1 SEP10 IMM A-DLLR G .84950
6/15 1 SEP10 IMM A-DLLR G .85020
6/15 1 SEP10 IMM A-DLLR G .85140
6/15 1 SEP10 IMM A-DLLR G .85240
6* 6* P & S 370.00 *
TOTAL COMM/FEE NET P&L 713.75
```

Day Trades 6/16

```
296VM 982 6/16/10 CQG 16 June
----BUY SELL------CONFIRMATI
WE HAVE MADE THIS DAY THE FOLLOWIN
6/16 1 SEP10 CBT T-BOND S 122.31
6/16 1 SEP10 CBT T-BOND S 123.00
6/16 1 SEP10 CBT T-BOND S 123.02
6/16 2 SEP10 CBT T-BOND S 123.01
6/16 1 SEP10 CBT T-BOND S 123.04
6/16 1 SEP10 IMM A-DLLR G .84960
6/16 1 SEP10 IMM A-DLLR G .84990
6/16 1 SEP10 IMM A-DLLR G .85010
```

brokerage firm to another. There's no excuse for losing money unnecessarily because you failed to understand how your broker reports your positions or what procedures you need to employ in order to enter, exit, cancel, and replace orders.

This brings me to the next topic, which is the use of orders designed to achieve specific goals for each trade. Before you make any trades, make certain you understand the following:

1. How to enter an order on your broker's trading platform

2. How to cancel an order on your broker's trading platform

3. How to replace an order on broker's trading platform

4. How to place a buy or sell at market order

FIGURE 17.3

Some day trades in futures on June 16 (continued)

```
6/16 1 SEP10 IMM A-DLLR G .85590
6/16 2 SEP10 IMM A-DLLR G .85610
6/16 1 SEP10 IMM A-DLLR G .85030
6/16 1 SEP10 IMM A-DLLR G .85060
6/16 1 SEP10 IMM A-DLLR G .85070
6/16 1 SEP10 IMM A-DLLR G .85230
6/16 1 SEP10 IMM A-DLLR G .85350
6/16 1 SEP10 IMM A-DLLR G .85400
6/16 1 SEP10 IMM A-DLLR G .85420
6/16 1 SEP10 IMM A-DLLR G .85550
6/16 1 SEP10 IMM A-DLLR G .85570
6/16 1 SEP10 IMM A-DLLR G .85590
6/16 2 SEP10 IMM A-DLLR G .85610
6/16 1 SEP10 IMM A-DLLR G .85620
14* 14* P & S 410.00 *
TOTAL COMM/FEE NET P&L 566.25
```

FIGURE 17.4

Some day trades in futures on June 24

```
6/24 1 SEP10 IMM A-DLLR G .85940
6/24 1 SEP10 IMM A-DLLR G .86080
6/24 2 SEP10 IMM A-DLLR G .86600
6/24 2 SEP10 IMM A-DLLR G .86640
6/24 2 SEP10 IMM A-DLLR G .86680
6/24 2 SEP10 IMM A-DLLR G .86700
6/24 12* 11* COMM/FEE 92.23-
TOTAL COMM 124.00-*
NFA .31-*
TOTAL COMM/FEE 124.31- *
----BUY SELL----PURCHASE & SALE
6/24 1 JUL10 CBT CORN S 3.43 3/4
6/24 1 JUL10 CBT CORN S 3.46 3/4
6/24 1 JUL10 CBT CORN S 3.45
6/24 1 JUL10 CBT CORN S 3.47 1/4
2* 2* P & S 87.50 *
6/24 2 SEP10 CBT T-NOTE S 121.07 1/2
6/24 2 SEP10 CBT T-NOTE S 121.08
2* 2* P & S 31.24 *
6/24 1 SEP10 IMM A-DLLR G .85880
6/24 1 SEP10 IMM A-DLLR G .85890
6/24 1 SEP10 IMM A-DLLR G .85930
6/24 1 SEP10 IMM A-DLLR G .85940
6/24 1 SEP10 IMM A-DLLR G .86050
6/24 2 SEP10 IMM A-DLLR G .86510
6/24 3 SEP10 IMM A-DLLR G .86650
6/24 1 SEP10 IMM A-DLLR G .86680
6/24 1 SEP10 IMM A-DLLR G .85910
6/24 1 SEP10 IMM A-DLLR G .85940
6/24 1 SEP10 IMM A-DLLR G .86080
6/24 2 SEP10 IMM A-DLLR G .86600
6/24 2 SEP10 IMM A-DLLR G .86640
6/24 2 SEP10 IMM A-DLLR G .86680
6/24 2 SEP10 IMM A-DLLR G .86700
11* 11* P & S 1,830.00 *
TOTAL COMM/FEE NET P&L 1,948.74
```

FIGURE 17.5

Some day trades in futures on August 27

```
   8/24/12 US DOLLARS FUNDS-Segregated Accounts US                  10,432.96
- - - -BUY SELL - - - - - -C O N F I R M A T I O N - - - - - - - - - - - - - -
WE HAVE MADE THIS DAY THE FOLLOWING TRADES FOR YOUR ACCOUNT AND RISK.
        1            DEC12 CBT SOYOIL      S            56.84
        1            DEC12 CBT SOYOIL      S            56.86
        2            DEC12 CBT SOYOIL      S            56.88
        1            DEC12 CBT SOYOIL      S            56.92
        1            DEC12 CBT SOYOIL      S            56.95
        2            DEC12 CBT SOYOIL      S            56.97
        1            DEC12 CBT SOYOIL      S            57.09
                 1   DEC12 CBT SOYOIL      S            56.88
                 1   DEC12 CBT SOYOIL      S            56.89
                 2   DEC12 CBT SOYOIL      S            56.96
                 1   DEC12 CBT SOYOIL      S            56.90
                 1   DEC12 CBT SOYOIL      S            57.00
                 1   DEC12 CBT SOYOIL      S            57.12
        9*       7*    COMM/FEE                   43.59-
               TOTAL COMM                          0.71 -*
               NFA                                  .32-*
               TRAN FEE                           32.96-*
               ROUTINGFEE                          1.60-*
             TOTAL COMM/FEE                        43.59-                    *
- - - -BUY SELL - - - - P U R C H A S E   &   S A L E - - - - - - - - - - -
 8/27   1            DEC12 CBT SOYOIL      S            56.84
 8/27   1            DEC12 CBT SOYOIL      S            56.86
 8/27   2            DEC12 CBT SOYOIL      S            56.88
 8/27   1            DEC12 CBT SOYOIL      S            56.92
 8/27   1            DEC12 CBT SOYOIL      S            56.95
 8/27   1            DEC12 CBT SOYOIL      S            56.97
 8/27            1   DEC12 CBT SOYOIL      S            56.88
 8/27            1   DEC12 CBT SOYOIL      S            56.89
 8/27            2   DEC12 CBT SOYOIL      S            56.96
 8/27            1   DEC12 CBT SOYOIL      S            56.98
 8/27            1   DEC12 CBT SOYOIL      S            57.00
 8/27            1   DEC12 CBT SOYOIL      S            57.12
        7*       7*                             P & S          291.00 *
             TOTAL COMM/FEE                     NET P&L        294.00 *
```

5. The difference between a stop and a stop limit order

6. How to place a stop loss order below the current market price

7. How to place a stop loss order above the current market price

8. How to place an OCO order (OCO = order cancels order)

9. When to use the appropriate order for each trade

10. When the markets you are trading open and close

11. The correct symbol or symbols for your broker's order entry platform

12. Your broker's policy with regard to order cancellations at the end of each day

13. Your broker's policy on good till canceled (GTC)

14. The "free-ride" rule in stock day trading

15. Any other aspects of order placement and order use that will be relevant to your trading

CONDITIONAL ORDERS

Because there are a number of different potential scenarios that can occur with a day trade, it is in the best interest of the active day trader to use conditional orders. As an example, consider the following: You buy 600 shares of stock at $20 per share. Your stop loss is $18.25. Your profit target is $21.10. If the profit target is hit, you want to sell 200 shares. If the 200-share profit target is hit, you want to change your stop loss from $18.25 to $20 per share on 200 shares. You want a trailing stop order on 200 shares locking in 75 percent of the open profit. If the trailing stop is hit, you want to change your breakeven stop to a 200-share trailing stop locking 75 percent of the profit. If neither of those alternatives is executed, you want to exit your position at market on close. Typically, such orders, given the numerous contingencies, would be difficult if not impossible to place unless you have the ability to enter conditional orders.

Some brokerage platforms offer the ability to enter conditional orders. However to do so effectively, you must link your brokerage account to a software program that will allow you to act on the various scenarios you may encounter. The program will connect to your trading account, which will then enter orders for you when the time comes based on your criteria. The program is instructed by you to "watch the markets" and then to act accordingly by placing orders automatically based on the fulfillment of your conditional criteria. Because the technology is changing constantly, I will not offer any suggestions regarding which programs to use for this purpose. Do know, however, that the ability to achieve multiple scenarios as a day trade or in different time frames is available and being improved all the time. Understand how these programs work, and use them profitably to enhance your day trading results significantly while reducing your workload.

HOW TO ACHIEVE ORGANIZATION

I have stressed the importance of being organized in your trading. The term *organization* is generic and covers a multitude of sins. What exactly does it mean to be organized as a day trader? For our purposes, organization means having focus and specificity.

Here are a few suggestions derived from my experience as a trader that, with some understandable variations, should apply to your day trading.

The first and most important aspect of organization is to know what your potential trades will be in the market or markets you are going to be trading that day, or on the next day, if your methodology allows you to do so. Have your list and charts ready, with the appropriate indicators on those charts. Additionally if you have a specific procedure that has allowed you to determine your entry price for these trades, you may also want to enter your orders accordingly. Such a procedure would apply, for example, to my MAC method.

Some traders do not wish to enter their orders prior to market opening. If that is the case, keep your list of potential trades ready and enter your orders based on your specific criteria as soon as the market is open. Use a checklist to make certain you have followed all necessary procedures correctly. After you have gained experience, your procedure will become quicker and more automatic. You don't need expensive software to do this. A simple checklist or Microsoft Excel file will do.

After you have entered the orders and your trades have been executed, track your trades using your broker's open position list or your own list. I find my broker's platform more efficient because the tracks are open profit or loss in real time and update with every change in price. Be aware that some platforms will have a 15- to 20-minute delay rather than tracking your trades in real time. Such a delay is unacceptable for the day trader; you will not be dealing with real-time data and will not know exactly where your trades stand.

If you are trading only one method with one or two stocks, this process will be much easier to implement and learn. I recommend starting out on a small scale. Day trading is the fastest game in town, and it's getting faster all the time. In order to compete effectively, you will also need to be fast.

Organization also pertains to knowing how much money you have available for your trades at any other point in time. As the day trader in stocks, you want to make certain that you're only using available funds for your trades. Some brokers will not permit you to trade on funds that have not cleared yet, or they will give you a warning. Prior to the end of each trading day, make sure you have closed out your positions accordingly and that you have canceled all orders that must be canceled. Do a final check of your positions and orders after the markets have closed to make certain you have executed all positions as necessary.

Check your account balances, open positions, and open orders every day, either at the end of the day, before the start of the day, or both. This will be especially important to you if you are trading many different stocks or commodities; your potential to make a costly mistake increases significantly with every additional position you have. Obviously if all you're doing is day trading and doing so by the rules, all positions must be closed down at the end of the day and there should be no open trades remaining.

YOUR TIME COMMITMENT TO DAY TRADING

I recently received the following letter from an individual who had read some of my books (the letter is quoted as is without any edits):

Hi Mr. Bernstein. I write to you out of frustration which has been caused by my ongoing and fervent commitment to the art and science of day trading. Virtually every day I spend up to five hours finding day trades, studying the markets, reading the news, digesting analyst opinions, and discussing potential trades with fellow traders in chat rooms. Unfortunately even after two years my valiant efforts have proven fruitless since I continue to lose money. In fact what adds insult to injury is the fact that there seems to be an inverse correlation between how much time I spend on the markets and how much money I'm making. More clearly stated, it's how much money I am losing as opposed to making. The more time I spend the more money I lose. As you can appreciate, this is a very frustrating situation which has driven me to the point of madness. Surely there must be an answer or some answers to my dilemma. Surely I am not the only one trapped in this Catch-22. If, as you have said in your books, great traders can be created and they are not born that way then I need some answers if you have them. What will it take to re-create me as a trader who can make money? What exactly is it that I'm doing wrong?

Signed HELP!

Here is part of my response to him:

Dear Help:
If you have indeed been spending all those hours and not getting any results or are, in fact, getting negative results, there is no doubt that you have gone astray and must be doing some terribly wrong things. You should have contacted me long ago; it is claimed that Einstein's definition of insanity is continuing to do something that doesn't work. From your letter you seem to be quite sane. I offer you the following suggestions without knowing all the details of your situation:

1. Focus on fewer stocks, and spend less time overall.

2. Focus on fewer methods, choosing only those with which you have been successful in the past.

3. Disregard the reports, recommendations, or stories that you see or hear on the business news; in fact, turn it off.

4. Don't waste your time in chat rooms. Why associate with other losers who seek only to promulgate their own ineffective ideas or to support stocks they already own?

5. Examine your losing trades, and determine why you lost. Were your losses a function of the trader or a function of the system? Did the system fail? Did the day trader fail?

If after making these changes you are still losing, contact me again and I will attempt to assist you.

Jake

One of the questions I am most often asked about day trading is how much time should be spent each day preparing for the next day. A subsidiary question is, how much time should be spent day trading each day? Without a doubt these are very important questions. Unfortunately there is no single, one-size-fits-all answer. Given the importance of these questions, I would like to be as clear with you as possible; success depends considerably on preparation time as well as the amount of time you spend trading.

Clearly the amount of time you spend preparing for each day will be a function of three things:

1. The greater the number of stocks, commodities, or Forex markets you follow or trade daily, the more time it will take you to plan your trades for the next day. As a new trader, I advise you to focus on quality, not quantity. My experience has been that initially one or two hours daily is more than enough to help you find and trade a sufficient number of markets profitably. Quality and focus are much more important than quantity.

2. If you are a day trader, you will spend more time in front of the computer daily during trading hours and less time preparing the day before.

3. The higher your frequency of trading, the more time it will take.

These are some of the factors that will facilitate success. As you can see, these are not mythical or mystical concepts. They are practical and mechanical. Ignore them and you will most certainly fail unless you have crazy good luck.

CHAPTER 18

Use the News—Don't Abuse the News

One of the mysteries of market life is a strange but frequent tendency for stock and other financial markets to move in a direction opposite from that which one would expect based on the news. Many traders, as well as the investing public, are surprised when negative news about a particular stock causes it to go up rather than down. Conversely there are many cases in which positive news causes the stock to move lower rather than higher. This is particularly frustrating as well as financially painful to individuals who react to the news by either buying or selling based on their expectation that the news will make them right. All too often investors who liquidate their holdings on a negative brokerage-house evaluation of their stock are frustrated and disappointed when the stock actually goes up after they have sold it.

Experienced traders are well acquainted with this phenomenon. The old expression "Buy the rumor, sell the news" is a dictum by which many experienced traders conduct their trading. Another well-worn expression is "Buy on anticipation and sell on realization." This, of course, is yet another way of saying that you may make more money by doing the opposite of what the news suggests as opposed to following the news.

In my view there is no mystery here. The news, in my experience, can be your friend as well as your foe. If our trading tools are effective, more often than not we will be positioned on the correct side of the market when news breaks. When a stock surges higher on positive news rather than add to our positions as day traders, we will use the emotional market response to our advantage by liquidating our positions. If we short a particular stock and our work is correct, we will take our profits as the stock plunges in response to the negative news.

In order to make this discussion an explanation of the news and its functionality as a day trading tool, we first have to define *news*. My broad definition is as follows:

Any report, any announcement, any story, whether disseminated by Internet, television, radio, fax, or e-mail, from any source, credible or not, that affects or has the potential to affect capital markets price movements either immediately or eventually.

I realize this is a very broad and general definition given that a literal interpretation covers every possible scenario. More specifically and for the purposes of this book, here is a list of items I consider to be news and therefore can be used in the various trading methodologies to be discussed later in this chapter:

1. Corporate earnings reports

2. Announcements of acquisitions or takeovers

3. Stock split announcements

4. Government reports issued either on a regular basis or unexpectedly, such as employment statistics, Federal Reserve minutes, GNP or GDP reports, Federal Reserve statements, crop reports, reports of Wells notices, and investigations

5. Specific recommendations either in print in the business media or on business radio or television

6. Specific comments on various stocks by well-known and/ or highly respected investors

7. Weather reports or news of weather developments that might affect business

8. "One off" events such as the attacks of September 11, assassinations such as that of Osama bin Laden and terrorist attacks on financial institutions or major government officials (prime minister, president, dictator, etc.)

9. Rumors about facts that may affect corporations or financial institutions, crops, or currency relationships

I realize this is a fairly extensive list, though I have attempted to be as specific as possible. If you have traded even for a short period of time, I'm certain you understand exactly what I'm referring to.

Now that we've taken a look at some more precise definitions of the term *news*, let's look at a few examples with charts that illustrate how the news can be used to advantage.

THE UNDERLYING PRINCIPLE

Joseph Granville, the legendary and often controversial stock market analyst and commentator, once quipped that "if it's obvious then it's obviously wrong." This was his way of saying that if you believe the action of a particular stock or in the market in general is obvious based on the facts, you are probably incorrect. The simple truth is that stock and futures markets are leading indicators. It has been said, most likely correctly, that the stock market leads the economy by as much as six months. If the stock market is moving up today, it is a reflection or forecast that the economy will be improving about six months from now. What would make this so?

The answer is very simple. Professional investors, money managers, and other savvy players make their money for themselves and their clients by anticipating what will happen. When they examine a corporate earnings report or evaluate economic trends, they do so in order to predict what will happen. Whether they do so using the fundamentals of the earnings, sales, crop conditions, or economic conditions, etc., or they use chart patterns, moving averages, and other forms of technical analysis, their goal is to make investments now and to capitalize on their profits later. By the time it becomes obvious to most investors that the trend of the market is up or down, that particular move is either over or close to being over. They had not noticed the trend, not believed the trend, waited for the trend to give them an opportunity to enter, or failed to see the big picture. When they are finally ready to accept that the market is moving in a given direction, the move is old, and most likely the professionals are getting out.

On the other hand, when stocks are declining, the tendency of most traders and investors is not to realize or admit to the fact that the market is declining. If they have invested money in a stock, they tend to become "married" to it, and often add the stock as it moves lower. Finally, when the news is at its worst, they tend to exit their positions, often selling to professional traders who are buying because they have done their homework and realize or expect the situation to improve.

What I have just stated is not theory but fact. Traders frequently talk about such market concepts as the Elliott wave or the Random Walk. The fact that the trading public is most often negative and selling at the bottom while being positive and buying at the top has been documented by my extensive studies of market sentiment. Although market sentiment and contrary opinion are beyond the scope of this book, they are fascinating as well as exceptionally useful tools for professional traders as well as for those who want to improve their market timing. As a point of information I offer Figure 18.1, showing small trader market sentiment plotted on a chart of S&P 500 futures. Take a few moments to examine the chart, then see my comments below.

Figure 18.1 shows the relationship between my Daily Sentiment Indicator (DSI) and the price of the S&P E-Mini futures. The DSI is a measure of small trader sentiment, which I have gathered every trading day since 1987. When the DSI is high (75 percent bullish sentiment or higher), this usually indicates that stocks are forming a top and that a decline is likely. This chart clearly indicates that a small trader is very positive, or bullish, at or close to the top of a market. This is the same reason that positive news tends to correlate closely with market tops. The arrow on my chart shows the relationship of DSI to price at the top of the market in March 2012.

Previous to this top the boxed area on the chart shows low market sentiment, which correlates with a significant lowering of prices. Uninformed investors or small traders were negative based on the news. Prices moved higher. The boxed area at the bottom of the chart in May 2012 correlates closely with a bottom in the market. From that point forward prices moved higher, and as of this writing the small trader, as assessed by the DSI, is not sufficiently positive or bullish on the market to correlate with an impending peak.

The evidence is strong in support of acting in a contrary fashion to the news. We want to investigate the possibility of using negative news as an opportunity to establish a long position and positive news as an opportunity to establish a short position.

FIGURE 18.1

Daily Sentiment Index vs. S&P E-Mini futures

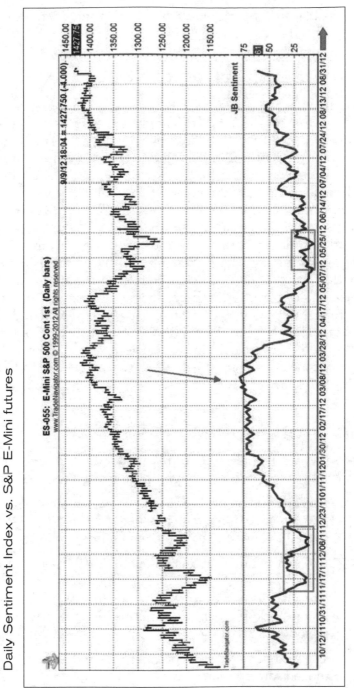

201

Let's take a look at some ground rules and examples for using this approach in day trading.

NEWS AS A SETUP

Using the news as a setup can be a very profitable and consistent approach to day trading. I gave specific examples of this approach *The Compleat Day Trader 2nd Edition*, citing what I termed the "CNBC day trade." This procedure involves using recommendations given by market experts on CNBC. I provided specific examples of how stocks tend to react, often violently and immediately, to buy or sell recommendations given by expert guests on CNBC business television station. Frequently recommendations would result in substantial and nearly immediate moves to the upside, which often ended very quickly. These dynamic and highly volatile moves can provide very profitable day trading opportunities when they are implemented correctly. For procedures on implementing the CNBC day trade, I refer you to that book. This type of day trade is a classic example of how to use the news in your favor by acting very quickly and entering positions consistent with the news, then exiting very quickly, while traders who are slower to respond are still buying.

THE PROCEDURE

Here is my step-by-step procedure for taking advantage of the news, followed by two specific examples of how the process works.

1. An earnings report is issued on a particular stock. The earnings report is interpreted as negative, as in the stock is expected to open lower in the next day's trading.

2. Do not assume that this will actually happen. Make a decision based on facts. If the earnings report is announced after the close of trading, examine the aftermarket response in the stock. If the stock responds lower and remains lower, the odds are that the stock will open lower the next day.

3. The next day check the preopening on the stock to see if it is indeed lower.

4. If the stock opened lower, go to your five-minute intraday chart and begin looking for buy signals based on the methods I discussed in previous chapters, including momentum divergence, moving average channel, and the gap trade.

5. If there is a signal to buy on any of these methods, implement the trade and follow through according to the rules.

6. Exit the trade by the end of the day.

7. Use the appropriate profit-maximizing strategy.

8. Remember above all that no setup and no trigger equals no trade.

Now let's examine an example of this approach.

On September 4, 2012, NFLX opened lower on negative news. If you bought on the opening and got out on the close of trading, you lost money. However, using the strategy described in this chapter, you would move to the one-minute or five-minute charts and use either of the procedures suggested. Figure 18.3 shows the one-minute NFLX with my momentum divergence setup and trigger. As you can readily see from the chart, waiting for the trigger to occur was the right procedure, while selling on the news and buying on the open would be the wrong procedure. Again I emphasize the importance of using a setup, trigger, and follow through as described in this book when taking advantage of trades based on news.

SUMMARY

The financial markets today are more news driven than ever before. The dissemination of news by Internet and broadcast media frequently creates a buying or selling frenzy based on the perceived significance and impact of the news. Electronic trading frequently sets off a chain reaction of buy and sell orders that by the end of the day may prove to have been nothing more than an emotional response or so-called "knee-jerk reaction." Day traders can take advantage of such developments by applying some of the ideas presented in this chapter. Depending on what type of news you listen to, you may have the opportunity for more trades on any given day than you can possibly handle.

FIGURE 18.2

NFLX lower opening on negative news

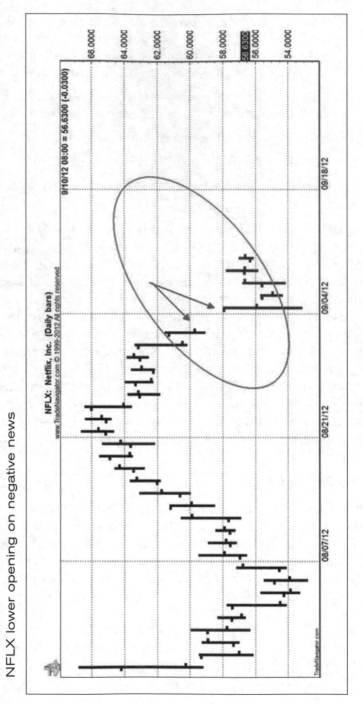

FIGURE 18.3

NFLX momentum divergence buy trigger and follow through

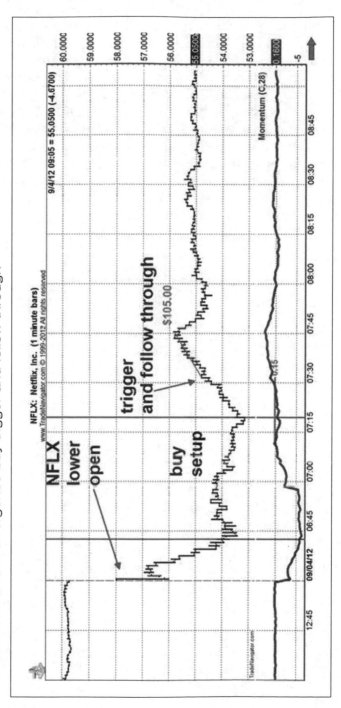

Computerized charting and trading software can be adjusted using filters and screens to specify certain criteria that will limit your potential day trades based on news as a function of various factors. Such factors would include price range, trading volume, size of the opening decline or price increase, underlying market trend, and, in futures, volume and open interest. You do not need many trades each day; you just need a few good ones. Before implementing my procedure, spend some time evaluating what I've told you and run through a number of scenarios, making certain you are familiar with the procedure and that it works for you. And if you find this approach is working for you, adapt it to your own level of position size, risk, and profit potential.

CHAPTER 19

A Case Study: Facebook

There is a world of difference between theory and practice. I can show you many different methods that have profit potential in day trading, but it is not until the methods are applied that you will fully understand their potential, as well as their limitations and nuances. A trader can possess powerful day trading tools, but those tools must be applied if profits are to be the result. Given that there are thousands of stocks, it is important to know which stocks to day trade, how to find them, and when to abandon them as your trading vehicles if they aren't working for you.

In Chapter 18 I discussed using the news as a method for day trading stocks. I showed you how to take advantage of knee-jerk or overreactions to such developments as earnings reports, geopolitical events, and purely financial events. By studying the markets and using your skill as a day trader, you will eventually gravitate toward certain stocks or commodities as your favorite day trading vehicles. My experience has taught me that it is better to consistently trade the same stocks or commodities than to jump around from one to another.

I always like to resolve confusion by forcing myself to deal only with what I know as opposed to what I do not know. Making decisions based on what you do not know might lead you to conclusions that have serious ramifications, as they did President Bush when he assumed Saddam Hussein had weapons of mass destruction. Had he known the actual as opposed to presumed facts, his response might have been very different, and that would have changed the course of history. Certainly a day trading decision does not have the ramifications that even approach the level of significance of the Bush decision; however I think I have made my point. Applying this logic, here are the facts I want to have at my disposal in making a day trade selection decision:

1. If I am using the gap trading method, I want to make certain I have selected only stocks that have an opening price gap. That's simple enough, and the computer can do it for us. The difficult part is that on any given day there may be several hundred stocks that open on a price gap. This poses a question: "Which one or ones should be traded?" In order to narrow down the choices, I recommend narrowing your filter selection criteria to the extent that your computer only searches for gap-opening trades in stocks that are trading between $10 and $50 a share and have traded an average of 5 million shares daily for the last 10 days. This will dramatically reduce the number of potential candidates and increase your focus as well as the probability of finding "good" trades. This is just an example, of course; you should make your own decision. You can restrict your search in other ways as well. For example, you can restrict your search only to S&P 100 stocks or optionable stocks or energy stocks, etc. As you can see, the goal is to limit your choices, not to expand them. In futures the task is easily achieved because there are only about 22 viable markets, and within that list there is considerable duplication.

2. If you are day trading swing trades based on MAC, the idea is the same as in selecting gap trades. Make a list and refer to it consistently, by which I mean every day, in order to find day trading opportunities. If this is not acceptable, have your filter apply the criteria, but I stress that your best results will be in having a predetermined list that you check for possible entries at the end of every day.

3. Many day traders lament the fact that they cannot consistently take advantage of the best opportunities. In order to do so sufficiently early in the inception of a significant day trade

opportunity, one would need to define and search for stocks meeting specific criteria. The success of such an approach would depend upon one's ability to define the proper search algorithms and/or the validity of those algorithms. And by the time certain opportunities present themselves, the moves may be over. This is particularly important in today's markets, which tend to make large moves very quickly.

4. Still another way to find potential day trading candidates is to regularly scan stocks that are in the news. The term *in the news* is general and vague. A more operational definition would be of assistance. Let's do just that.

MY APPROACH TO THE SELECTION PROCESS

I have found that one of the best ways to select day trading stocks is by picking stocks that are in the news. My reference above to the term *in the news* covers a multitude of sins. I will narrow the definition. At any point in time there are stocks or commodity sectors, as well as currency markets, that for one reason or another are being talked about very actively either in print, broadcast, or Internet media. These may be stocks that have particularly good or bad news, are takeover candidates, or are the subject of investigations, inquiries, or surprise earnings—or lack thereof. In the commodity markets they may be markets that are particularly sensitive to weather or political factors or financial considerations. One need only listen to the news or read some media or Internet reports for several days in order to determine which these stocks may be. Typically such stocks present numerous day trading opportunities, given that they are affected by many developments during the day. The cast of characters changes frequently, with some stocks being perennial favorites and others being ephemeral players. Regardless, it is fairly easy to find and trade them accordingly. But, there's more to it than meets the eye.

First you have to find your list of candidates, and next you have to determine whether to buy or sell them. I've already described these steps. The next step, of course, is to apply' the methods discussed in this book. Using the stock of Facebook (FB) as a case study, you will be able to extrapolate to other stocks and commodity markets that are in the news.

THANK YOU, MARK ZUCKERBERG

Even if you are the most passive of investors and not at all interested in speculation or day trading, it would have been difficult if not impossible for you to escape being exposed to the Facebook initial public offering media hype. For weeks on end, Facebook was every-where. CNBC discussed Facebook many times daily. The blogo-sphere was awash with every manner and sort of opinion regarding everything from the price at which it would go public, how quickly or slowly it would rise thereafter, and whether it was a candidate for much higher prices or the stock would plunge after the IPO. Every-one had an opinion. Several days before Facebook went public, there were reports that many parents who were trying to encourage their children to get involved in the stock market approached this task by suggesting they buy Facebook stock, given that they were Facebook addicts. Not only were the media and Internet drowning in Facebook news, but opinions varied from the most conservative to the most extreme. Given the media circus, Facebook was a stock of interest to me.

What did I know about the stock? I knew that I had no inter-est in revealing my innermost thoughts, feelings, struggles, lunch menu, travel itinerary, or friends on Facebook. Unfortunately one of my employees created a Facebook page for me, thinking it would be a good way to make my work better known to the public. Again, I had no interest and never once updated my Facebook page.

I also knew that Facebook was so aggressively promoted and advertised for so many months that it was not a given that Facebook would soar on its initial public offering. I remembered fondly and frequently the words of Joe Granville, who had told me so many times that if it's obvious, it's obviously wrong. Then again, I also had had my doubts about LinkedIn, which did perform dramati-cally higher. I never traded LinkedIn.

What else did I know? I knew that at some point on the IPO day Facebook would be worth trading. I knew I did not want to be a buyer or seller immediately on the opening; I wanted to give it time to develop a setup in the trigger based on my methods and then take action based on those triggers.

I also knew that the IPO day would be one of great volatility as prices jumped back and forth in a fairly large range and with great frequency. This was particularly interesting to me because volatility is the lifeblood of many day trading opportunities.

Knowing what I knew and not paying attention to what I didn't know, I was ready to trade Facebook on the IPO day. Remember that my choice of this stock was based on the fact that without a doubt it was in the news.

May 18, 2012

Facebook stock started trading with great fanfare after a few delays on May 18, 2012. By the end of the day a new chapter in IPO debacles had been written. None of that interested me. What did interest me, and what should interest you, is the procedure I used in determining whether and how to trade in the stock.

One of my office associates was also watching the stock, and we consulted on the following trade. We allowed the stock time to establish an intraday trend using the two-minute price chart, which appears below in Figure 19.1.

As you can readily observe, Facebook stock dropped immediately after opening for trading and continued its decline from about $45 per share to $38 per share. At that time we did not have sufficient data to form a chart indicator for Facebook. However, as the minutes passed, we were able to run a MAC indicator. There was insufficient data to run a Williams AD/MA indicator. When Facebook presented to complete consecutive price bars above the moving average high, I concluded that the stock had temporarily made a low; therefore I was keen to buy at the MAC low. An order was placed to buy, and in the ensuing volatility a price execution at 38.02 was acquired. This price execution was way beyond anything we expected. It was a gift. Figure 19.2 shows the two bars above the MAC by indication, and the arrow shows where the trade was filled.

Figure 19.2 shows the MAC by signal (two consecutive bars above the price moving average high), the entry point (arrow at the bottom of the chart), and the approximate exit area when prices pulled back.

Figure 19.3 shows the trade confirmations for this very quick trade in Facebook.

FIGURE 19.1

Two-minute chart of Facebook (FB) on the IPO day

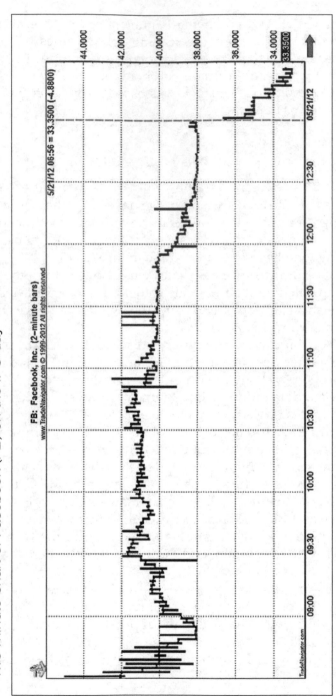

FIGURE 19.2

Two-minute Facebook MA

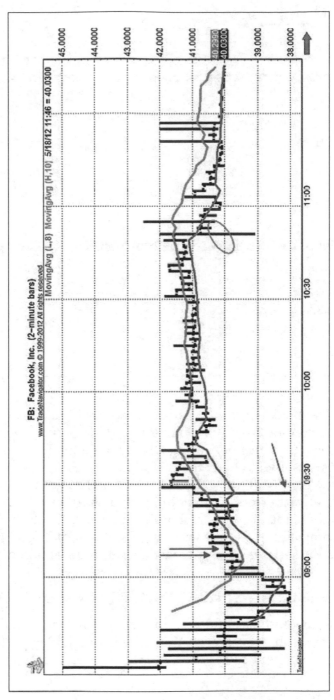

FIGURE 19.3

Trade confirmations for the Facebook transaction

Trade Confirmation				
I 17471				Print

Trade Date | **Action** | **Quantity** | **Price** | **Amount**
05/18/2012 | Bought | | 38.02 |

Security Description FACEBOOK INC CLASS A COMMON STOCK
EXECUTED 100% AGENCY. WE MAKE A MARKET IN THIS ISSUE
CLIENT ENTERED.
ML ACTED AS AGENT.
SOLD PURSUANT TO REGISTRATION STATEMENT OR WHERE A PROSPECTUS IS
OTHERWISE REQUIRED. ACCESS DOC AT
WWW.IPROSPECTUSDIRECT.COM/BAML

SEE ABOVE FOR TRANSACTION DETAILS

Processing Fee

Transaction Fee

Accrued Interest/Dividend

Net Amount

Trade Confirmation

-17471

Trade Date | **Action** | **Quantity** | **Price** | **Amount**
05/18/2012 | Sold | | 40.31 |

Security Description FACEBOOK INC CLASS A COMMON STOCK
EXECUTED 100% AGENCY. WE MAKE A MARKET IN THIS ISSUE
CLIENT ENTERED.
ML ACTED AS AGENT.

Facebook went on to trade in a more subdued fashion until the end of the day. From that point forward, Facebook stock continued its precipitous decline, during which it became the stock a majority of analysts love to hate, the whipping boy that personified everything wrong with the U.S. stock market. The exchange was vilified for "software errors" in handling the initial transactions. Threats of lawsuits made the news practically every day. Commentators piled on, complaining about everything Facebook did wrong, including Mark Zuckerberg's T-shirt, marriage, attitude, and demeanor.

FACEBOOK: THE STOCK THEY LOVE TO HATE

As Facebook stock continued to drop almost daily, analysts, prognosticators, bloggers, and other self-proclaimed experts pounded the stock relentlessly, even to the extent that some analysts predicted the company would go broke. They complained about everything from the chart pattern of the stock to its inability to monetize mobile applications, going so far as to suggest that insiders manipulated the IPO to cash out as much of their money as possible.

I watched the parade of negativity knowing that one day, sooner rather than later, Facebook would become so unpopular, so hated, so neglected, that the contrarian point of view would be best. This was yet another example of how negative news led me to my next Facebook trade. Because sentiment was so negative, because the chart pattern was so negative, because momentum divergence began to develop, I focused on Facebook as a potential recovery candidate and a buy trade. I knew that once the stock bottomed, the odds were substantial that the ensuing rally would be more than just a one-day event. Accordingly I made the decision to buy Facebook on the next momentum divergence day trade trigger and hold it for more than just a day trade if possible. However, in the interim I expected that there could be several intraday trades on the long side. Why? The answer is simple: Sentiment was so negative, short sellers were so abundant, negative news was an almost hourly event, and the stock refused to continue its sharp decline. Knowing what I knew about market sentiment, both positive and negative, I saw this situation as the exact opposite of what preceded the decline after the IPO.

Looking at Some Charts

Figure 19.4 shows the daily chart of Facebook, along with my momentum 28 indicator. I observed that as prices continued to go down, momentum began to go up. I've marked these two points with arrows. I also observed that the daily price range (area shown by rectangle) began to narrow, which suggested to me that buyers and sellers were coming into balance and that a low was likely. Figure 19.5 shows the momentum divergence by setup and trigger, which allowed me to buy the stock and exit several days later at a profit. This was not a day trade; however there were a number of instances prior to this low where intraday indicators turned bullish, allowing for some potentially profitable day trades.

FIGURE 19.4

Facebook daily chart showing price moving lower with momentum moving higher as a precedent condition to a low

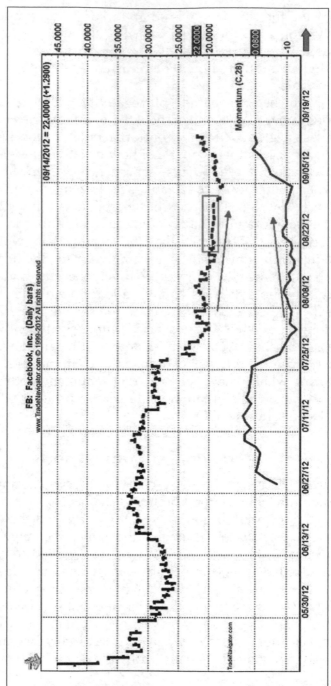

FIGURE 19.5

Facebook daily chart showing momentum divergence by trigger and follow through

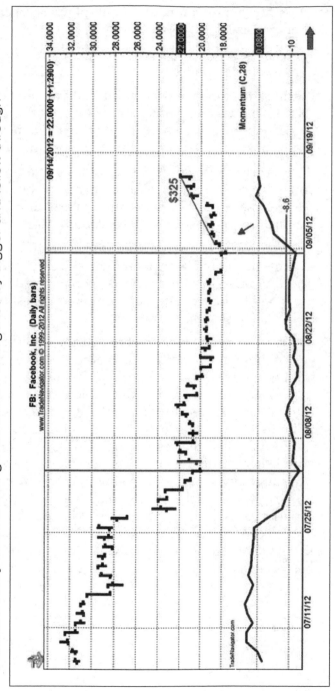

My intention in presenting the details of my Facebook transactions is to emphasize the following points:

1. There are several ways in which we can find stocks or commodities to day trade.

2. I wanted to emphasize the point that you are far better off specializing than you are generalizing. By this I mean that you cannot be everywhere all the time; you may lose your focus, make mistakes, and ultimately lose money.

3. If you work from a preselected group of markets and choices, you will be consistent in your performance, but you will not catch as many opportunities, particularly in situations that are relatively rare, such as the Facebook case.

4. One way to find day trade candidates that are likely to make extreme moves one way or another, not only on an intraday basis but on a short-term one, is by paying attention to the news and being a contrarian. Some of my best trades have been made using that approach.

5. You can use a combination of the various approaches I suggested, but remember that the methods I have presented in this book are relatively simple and easy to implement. In the futures and Forex markets, your choices are limited, which is a good thing. In the stock market your choices are virtually unlimited, and that's a bad thing. In order to compensate for the unlimited choices, you need to narrow your selection criteria in accordance with the suggestions I have provided. My suggestions are by no means the only ways in which to narrow your field of possible choices. Once you have experience as a day trader, you will gravitate naturally toward certain types of markets that meet your criteria both from a financial-risk perspective as well as a psychological perspective.

CONCLUSION

Although I have done my best to provide you with specific, objective, and highly detailed methods and illustrations for day trading, the ultimate implementation is up to you. My job is an easy one. I simply give illustrations and examples of what I have developed during four decades of trading. The difficult job is now yours. You are the one who must implement the methods with discipline, consistency, and persistence.

The task that awaits all day traders, whether they are new to the game or veterans, is not getting easier; rather it is becoming more difficult due to the intense competition that continues to grow minute by minute. Your competition is not only other day traders; it is primarily from the professional side of the business. You are competing with hedge funds, high-frequency traders, and seasoned veterans. It is not necessarily true that you will be wrong if they are right. It is true, however, that their timing and ability to implement trades for both entry and exit may be faster and more efficient than yours. They pay lower commissions than you and may also be privy to information you do not have. Whether they obtain such information legally or otherwise is not the issue; information will always be available for those who are able to pay for it or scheme for it.

In addition to methods and procedures on the finer details of day trading, I have included substantial material on the do's and don'ts of day trading, as well as on the psychology or behavior of day trading. By far and away the behavioral side of the equation has been and will continue to be the weakest link in the chain. Without control of emotions, iron discipline, perfect organization, and sufficient starting capital, nothing consistent in the way of profits from day trading can ever be achieved.

Should you find that you are spending many hours each day either day trading and/or researching your day trades for the next day and losing money or barely making money—or profiting to the extent that you could be working at a fast-food restaurant to achieve the same end—you are clearly heading in the wrong direction and are fulfilling Einstein's definition of insanity if you keep on doing the same thing. Change what you are doing. Examine it in detail, by looking closely at the process. See where you are going wrong. Understand where you are making your mistakes. Analyze the sequence of your trading. In order to do so, you will need to have good records of what you have done, so make sure you keep a diary or log of every trade you make, why you made it, the entry rule, the exit rule, the price entered, the price exited, and all relevant details of your decision-making process.

Finally, remember that the technology of day trading continues to accelerate geometrically. There will be many new tools and approaches. There will be great claims and promises, though most will be specious and hollow. Be careful. Be consistent in your trades. Begin with sufficient capital. Trade less, not more. Be systematic. Follow your rules. Maximize profits. And if you are lost, perhaps I can point you in the right direction. Send me an e-mail; if your question is simple and direct, I will do my best to answer you. Please keep in mind that I get many e-mails every day, and I'm not able to answer all of them as quickly as I'd like. But if your e-mail is short, direct, to the point, and constructive, I will attempt to answer you within several days. My address is jake@trade-futures.com.

Thank you for taking the time to read this book, and may you prosper through its methods, ideas, and procedures. If I have changed the fortunes of one trader for the better, I will be satisfied. If I have not changed your fortunes but at least have given you food for thought that ultimately leads you in the direction of improved profits, I will have done my job.

INDEX